3.16.77

THE SECRETS
OF
OUR SEXUALITY

OTHER BOOKS FROM
THE CONTINENTAL CONGRESS ON THE FAMILY

It's O.K. to Be Single
Make More of Your Marriage
Facing the Future: Church and Family Together
Living and Growing Together: The Christian Family Today

THE SECRETS
OF
OUR SEXUALITY

Role Liberation for the Christian

Gary R. Collins, editor

WORD BOOKS, Publisher • Waco, Texas

THE SECRETS OF OUR SEXUALITY

ISBN #0-87680-847-X
Library of Congress catalog card number: 76-2865
Printed in the United States of America

CONTENTS

THE SECRETS
OF
OUR SEXUALITY

Introduction

When God created the human race, he could have made us unisex creatures—but he did something better. He made us male and female, gave us different bodies, added some hormones, and told us how to enjoy sex.

Then something went wrong. Our ancient parents decided to rebel against God and we've been having problems, including sex problems ever since. We've used sex to satisfy our selfish animal instincts, to break up marriages, to destroy feelings of self-worth and to sell everything from automobiles and newspapers to hamburgers and bowling balls. Our abuse of sex has led to confusion, guilt, tension, manipulation, exploitation, and a host of other human miseries. Ignoring clear biblical teachings, innumerable people—even Christians—have convinced themselves that in the area of sex, "If it feels good, we should do it!" Extramarital sex, premarital intercourse, homosexual sex, prostitution and what we used to call perversion, are all becoming accepted as part of our way of life, so much so that even Christians are no longer surprised or shocked by sexual looseness of our society.

In the midst of this sexual revolution Christians too often have been confused about sexual roles, not sure what kinds of sexual behavior are acceptable, afraid that we might enjoy sex too much, reluctant to talk about such taboo subjects as masturbation or oral-genital stimulation, uncertain about how our male and female bodies work, hesitant to tell our children the truth about sex, worried lest our kids get wrong ideas about sex, confused about the morality of homosexuality and reluctant to speak out against the sexual degradation that permeates our society.

In the following pages, nine different writers have tried to deal with these topics of sexuality in a straightforward and helpful manner. Each of these chapters was prepared originally for presentation at the Continental Congress of the Family, a major gathering of evangelical leaders, planned and directed by J. Allan Petersen, President of Family Concern, Inc. of Omaha, Nebraska. Following the Congress in 1975, the chapters were revised for publication in this volume.

The first four chapters of the book deal with male and female roles. Letha Scanzoni begins by discussing unisex and questioning whether men and women should be assigned specific duties in a society or expected to show certain personality traits, solely because of their sex. John Scanzoni, Letha's sociologist husband, carries the discussion further by considering the place of women in the Bible and by arguing that both men and women should be free to develop their God-given talents, abilities and gifts. In the next two chapters, Mary Van Leeuwen and Gary Collins discuss what it means to be feminine and masculine in an age when femininity and masculinity have become confused and confusing terms.

The last six chapters consider the physical side of sex. Following Harry Hollis's discussion of the real meaning of sex, physician Ed Wheat describes the physiology of sex and gives some practical suggestions for improving the joys of sexual intercourse. Dennis Kinlaw and Guy Charles then discuss homosexuality, first from a biblical point of view, and then from the perspective of one who has spent most of his life as a practicing homosexual. Letha Scanzoni next discusses sex education including parental response to the big question: "How does daddy put the little sperm cell into mommy?" The book concludes with David Seamand's insightful discussion of masturbation and premarital sex, followed by his positive, enthusiastic statement about sexual fulfillment as God, who created sex, meant it to be.

Sex has been misused by all of us, but it is something which God meant for us to enjoy, not to abuse. The chapters in this book and the study guide which follows are meant to stimulate your thinking; to cause a reevaluation of your views about sex, to help you examine what it means to be male or female today, and to present sex in a biblical perspective. Hopefully, the book will accomplish one other purpose—to help you better accept, appreciate and enjoy your own sexuality, praising God that he made us male and female.

—GARY R. COLLINS

A Christian View
of Men's and Women's Roles
in a Changing World
Part I

1

Women and Men: How Different Should We Be?

Letha Scanzoni

Several years ago while looking through an alumni magazine, I was rather startled to see a headline announcing: "Betty Crocker Earns Ph.D." Sure enough, the woman who for fifteen years had represented General Mills in promotional work and whose neat signature appeared on cake-mix boxes and cookie-recipe pamphlets was now beginning a retirement career in communications. After being awarded a doctorate by New York University, she was asked about her future. "One thing is certain," she said. "I'll spend as little time in the kitchen as possible. I hate to cook."[1]

More recently, the news media carried reports of the first woman in history to reach the top of Mount Everest. For *anyone* to scale the world's highest peak is no mean achievement; for a five-foot, ninety-two-pound *woman* to do so surely should dispel those old ideas about the alleged weakness of the female sex! Mrs. Junko Tabei, mother of a three-

---

Letha Scanzoni is a professional writer and the author of six books, including *All We're Meant to Be*, coauthored with Nancy Hardesty, and *Men, Women, and Change*, coauthored with her husband John Scanzoni. She is much in demand as a speaker on subjects related to marriage. Letha and John Scanzoni have two sons.

year-old daughter, trained for nearly three years to take part in the expedition. Her proud husband told reporters that she had financed the five-thousand-dollar trip through her own earnings as a piano teacher.[2]

Stories such as these can leave little doubt in our minds: women's roles are changing, and so are men's. We read of rugged athletes who enjoy knitting and needlepoint. Men are adept at cooking and baking and are writing books about it. Large numbers of husbands enroll with their wives in natural childbirth classes and fight hospital policies which bar fathers from the delivery room. Men want to share the special moments of childbearing and childrearing. Increasingly, men are realizing that they've been cheated out of a tremendously rich aspect of life because older ideas about male roles have kept them so busy with breadwinning that they have had little time with their families. Many men are wondering if it has really been so wise after all to insist that "woman's place is in the home" because that notion seems to carry with it another side, "Man's place isn't in the home." Somehow that doesn't seem fair. At the same time, many women feel hindered from living up to their full potential. To say, "Man's place is in the world," has all too often implied that woman's place isn't there.

In the past, both customs and laws have reinforced such ideas which are being questioned and challenged in today's changing world. Many perplexed Christians grope for the security of some prior time that in retrospect seems ideal— a time when sex roles weren't blurred and everybody knew his or her place. As television's Archie Bunker sings, "Girls were girls and men were men. Those were the days!"

IN THE BEGINNING

When Jesus was asked about men and women and how God intended them to relate to one another, he too suggested going back in time—*really* back, to the very beginning. The Pharisees had come to him with a question about divorce; and in his reply, Jesus said, "Have you not read that he who made them from the beginning made them male and female, and said, 'For this reason a man shall leave his father and mother and be joined to his wife, and the two shall become one flesh'?" (Matt. 19:4–5, RSV).

Jesus specifically indicates God's purpose in creating the human race in two sexes. God "made them male and female," Jesus said, and *"for this reason . . .* the two shall become one." Joined in marriage, the woman and man could be fruitful and multiply and share in the Creator's work, carrying out his mandate through bringing new human lives into the world.

However, both men and women were told to share in God's work in still another way—by having dominion over the works of God's hands (Ps. 8) and by subduing the earth. According to Genesis 1:27 and 5:1–2, human beings—both male and female—were created by God and in his image. According to Genesis 1:28, both male and female were commissioned by God to have responsibility in both areas of life —the family and work in the outside world. Labor was not divided by gender.

GENDER ROLES

The overall title of this chapter and the next, "A Christian View of Men's and Women's Roles in a Changing World," raises two important questions: Exactly what are roles anyway? And what are gender roles (or sex roles)?

Sociologists use the term *roles* to apply to the parts people are expected to play in human society, somewhat as an actor plays a part in a drama. The actor studies a prewritten script and then comes on the stage to enact the role of a particular character. What he says and what he does fits with what is expected of him *as long as he is in that role*. Offstage, he may be altogether different. Similarly, in everyday life, people act according to roles, that is, they fulfill social expectations for behavior considered appropriate to their particular role at the time—doctor, pastor, salesperson, teacher, student, friend, parent, or whatever.

The roles we play in life come about in two ways. Some are *achieved* (such as when a person wins an election and takes on the role of mayor or obtains the necessary credentials for a profession and assumes the role of a lawyer or psychiatrist). Other roles are *ascribed* on the basis of characteristics over which a person has no control, such as race or age or sex. For example, in a caste society divided by race, a person would be assigned either a privileged role or a subservient role simply by having been born into a certain racial category. Abilities or achievement would have nothing to do with the assigned position and the behaviors expected to go with it.

Gender roles are ascribed. Persons have no control over whether they are born male or female. Yet, regardless of individual abilities, interests, and proclivities, persons have been expected according to their sex to fill roles laid down for them in advance, just as surely as the actor is expected to order his behavior according to the prewritten script. Males are expected to behave one way and females another, and they are taught these expected behaviors or gender roles from childhood. This idea is being called into question today.

However, the questioning isn't really new. In the late 1700s, a sea captain's daughter, writing under the pen name "Constantia," published a series of pamphlets calling for equal educational opportunities for women. As a Christian, she was convinced that the more training a woman had, the better she would be equipped to utilize her talents for God. Yet women were barred from higher education. (Some clergymen claimed that education would just make women restless and make them want to leave their husbands. Furthermore, they said, women were told in the Bible that if they had questions they should simply ask their husbands at home. So why would they need an education?) Constantia wrote:

> Is it reasonable that a candidate for immortality, for the joys of heaven, an intelligent being, who is to spend eternity in contemplating the works of Deity, should at present be so degraded as to be allowed no other ideas than those which are suggested by the mechanism of a pudding, or the sewing of the seams of a garment?[3]

In the middle of the nineteenth century, Lucy Stone spoke out similarly. Referring to the words of abolitionist Wendell Phillips who had said, "The best and greatest thing one is capable of doing, that is his sphere," Lucy Stone spoke up for women's rights:

> I have confidence in the Father to believe that when He gives us the capacity to do anything He does not make a blunder. Leave women, then, to find their sphere. And do not tell us before we are born even, that our province is to cook dinners, darn stockings, and sew on buttons. . . . I know not what you believe of God, but I believe He gave yearnings and longings to be filled, and that He did not mean all our time should be devoted to feeding and clothing the body.[4]

But we could go back much further than the eighteenth and nineteenth centuries to find complaints about assigning or denying privileges on the basis of sex. The Old Testament Book of Numbers tells the story of a man who died leaving five daughters and no sons, which meant that the family name and inheritance would go elsewhere. The daughters felt this was unfair, and they agitated for justice. " 'Why should the name of our father be taken away from his family, because he had no son? Give to us a possession.'

. . . Moses brought their case before the Lord. And the Lord said to Moses, 'The daughters of Zelophehad are right; you shall . . . cause the inheritance of their father to pass to them' " (Num. 27:4–7, RSV).

WHY SHOULD GENDER MATTER?

Increasingly, behavioral scientists are showing that the sexes have far more in common than they have differences. Thus, today perhaps as never before, ascribed roles on the basis of gender seem totally out of place. *Individual* capabilities and achievements and personalities are what count, not one's membership in a certain social category labeled "black" or "white" or "male" or "female"—at least ideally. It puzzles me that so many Christians find this threatening and, in some cases, are calling for a more extreme and rigid segregation of sex roles than ever before. At a time when we as women and men could be coming so much closer together because of all that we are finding we have in common, we are being told by some that we are so radically different we must each make sure we keep in our "proper place." Perhaps it will help to examine what is involved in gender roles and the behavior expectations associated with them.

In speaking of differences between the sexes, persons generally are not referring to biology (because everybody knows about these physical differences which make possible reproduction); rather, they are thinking of assumed differences in appropriate *activities* and appropriate *attributes.*

GENDER-ASSIGNED ACTIVITIES

Many persons simply take for granted that there is a natural division of labor according to sex. A man is assigned the role of family provider; a woman is assigned the role of caretaker of the home and children. Certain tasks are designated as "women's work," other tasks as "men's work." What is often overlooked, however, is that there is no universal consensus about what *is* "women's work" (except child-bearing) or "men's work." Persons aren't programed by nature to gravitate toward certain activities according to sex; they *learn* what is expected of them according to their particular society's ideas of gender roles. Anthropologists have found some tribes in which weaving or pottery making is exclusively men's work; in other tribes these activities are exclusively women's work. In still other tribes, both men and women perform these tasks. Similar patterns are found with regard to such activities as house building, harvesting crops, manufacturing leather products, and so on.[5] If dividing labor a certain way according to sex was simply "natural," we wouldn't find such differences.

According to Genesis 1, there was no gender-linked division of labor at creation, but some Christians feel that Genesis 3 commands such a pattern. After sin entered the world through the couple's disobedience to God, the woman was told that she would labor in bringing forth children while the man was told he would labor in bringing forth food from the soil. It seems to me, however, that the main point in this passage is that sin not only has consequences for men and women in their relationship with God but also in their relationship with each other. The husband would "lord it over" the wife (Gen. 3:16, JB). The perfect partnership of Genesis 1 and 2 was spoiled, and the effects of sin would be seen in both areas mentioned earlier— family life and the world of work. Remember, God wasn't showing Adam and Eve what *should* be but rather what *would* be as a result of the Fall. As Christians we are not called to perpetuate the sinful order but to live in newness of life in Christ Jesus and in the redemption order that he makes possible.

At any rate, I don't think we can use Genesis 3 to insist that the care of home and children belongs exclusively or primarily to women and that caring for the affairs of the world is the province of men only. The Bible contains numerous examples of godly women with outside careers: Deborah who judged Israel and led an army, Lydia the businesswoman, Priscilla the tentmaker, the "virtuous woman" or "good wife" of Proverbs 31 who managed the household finances and made major purchases and also had her own garment-manufacturing business. The Bible also speaks of men in terms of tasks that are often labeled "women's work." Jesus cooked fish and served breakfast to the disciples in a postresurrection appearance (John 21). Paul compared himself to a nurse gently caring for her children or a father exhorting or encouraging them (1 Thess. 2:7, 11). Jesus compared himself to a hen longing to gather her chicks. Both the Old and New Testaments urge fathers as well as mothers to be involved in training their children.

In Colonial America, the Puritans gravely exhorted children to find their "particular calling"—the vocation God had for each one. Boys were told they could discern God's will by paying attention to the talents God had bestowed upon them and through their own interest in and inclination toward a certain occupation. Adults encouraged them in their aptitudes for farming, or skilled trades, or one of the professions such as the ministry, teaching, or medicine; and they were apprenticed and schooled accordingly. But girls were given apprenticeships in domestic work only. Parents, teachers, and clergy simply took for granted that God's "particular calling" for each girl was exactly the same— homemaking and motherhood.[6] No one seemed to consider applying the same reasoning to girls as was applied to boys, namely, that God directs us in our occupational choices through the talents he bestows and through our own interests in particular careers.

Yet, according to the Scriptures, the Holy Spirit apportions gifts "to each individually as he wills." There is nothing said about limitations according to gender, and there is no room here for ascribed roles. Each person *as an individual* is responsible to use the abilities God gives—regardless of one's sex (1 Cor. 12; Rom. 12). Women and men alike are God's stewards and responsible to him to use the talents he places in our hands; we have no right to bury them in a napkin (Luke 19:20; Matt. 25:25).

I hope that we as Christian parents today won't make the same mistake the Puritans did. Through the toys we give them, the personal examples (role models) to which we expose them, and the books we place in their hands, let's help and challenge our daughters so they won't be limited to the idea that the domestic side of life is the *only* choice open to them. And let's help our sons see that personal aptitudes and interests should guide them in various activities instead of being bound by sex-role stereotypes ("Boys don't do that." "That's sissy."). I wonder, for example, why parents are often so alarmed when a little boy wants to play with dolls. Why can't this be viewed as something good—rehearsal for parenthood in adulthood—as we view it for girls?

GENDER-ASSIGNED ATTRIBUTES

Not only are certain activities considered to belong to one sex or the other, but so are certain personal characteristics. Men are thought to be by nature aggressive, rational, courageous, strong, and tough; women are thought to be nonassertive, nurturant, tender, more passive than active, and intuitive. However, many behavioral scientists are pointing out that these qualities may be and should be found in all human beings. We are wrong to label them "masculine" or "feminine" and train males to develop one set of such qualities and females to develop another. Men are often afraid to be tender, poetic, or to admit weakness because they think this is to "act feminine." Women are often afraid to display strength and assertiveness because they fear it means they are being "unfeminine" or "masculine." As a result, all of us are denying our full humanness.

The whole idea of labeling characteristics "masculine" or "feminine" is patently unscriptural. Otherwise, we'd have to call the fruit of the Spirit a list of feminine qualities (Gal. 5:22); admonitions to "fight the good fight," be strong, courageous, and put on the whole armor of God would have to be called masculine. Yet all these qualities—from meekness to being more than conquerors—are expected of all Christians and have nothing to do with whether we are male or female. Jesus wept, as did other men who weren't afraid to display sorrow or affection (John 11:33–36; Acts 20:37; 2 Tim. 1:4). And just as there are many examples of tenderness in men, there are abundant examples of rationality, courage, and assertiveness in women described throughout the Bible.

Sociologists speak of two sides of life. The *instrumental side* is concerned with mastery, rationality, and getting things done, and the *expressive side* is concerned with feelings and relating to people. These terms seem preferable to "masculine" and "feminine" because to have a rich, full life, persons of both sexes need to be instrumental (task-oriented) and expressive (people-oriented). These ideas also relate to recent psychological findings about the working of the human brain, with one side functioning in logical, rational, linear thinking, and the other side functioning intuitively, symbolically, and making analogies and metaphors.[7]

FEARS ABOUT "UNISEX"

Many Christians fear that doing away with clearly defined sex roles in terms of gender-assigned activities and attributes will confuse children about their sexual identity. Psychohormonal researchers John Money and Anke Ehrhardt allay such fears by reminding us of the natural differences that cannot be erased—hair grows on men's faces, women have breasts, the voice pitches of the sexes differ. And of course, men impregnate and women give birth. There is no denying obvious biological differences between males and females; God designed us this way and pronounced it very good. But from both Genesis and the answer of Jesus in Matthew 19, it seems that marriage and reproduction (being "one flesh" and being "fruitful") were the primary reasons for sexual differences. Since these differences are obvious, I see no need to add to them by arbitrarily assigning certain activities and attributes to one sex or the other. As Drs. Money and Ehrhardt write:

> Provided that a child grows up to know that sex differences are primarily defined by the reproductive capacity of the sex organs, and to have a positive feeling of pride in his or her own genitalia and their ultimate reproductive use, then it does not much matter whether various child-care, domestic, and vocational activities are or are not interchangeable between mother and father. It does not even matter if mother is a bus driver and daddy a cook.[8]

The term *unisex* implies that there would be one sex only, but God created us as two sexes. In matters of physical sex, let us rejoice in our differences. In all other areas of life, let us cultivate what we have in common and work together, women and men, as partners in the service of our God. Gender roles are changing, but let's not permit misinformation and misunderstanding to cause us to resist the good that these changes can bring about. What needs to be stressed is not *uni-sex* but *uni-ty*. "There is neither male nor female; for you are all one in Christ Jesus" (Gal. 3:28, RSV).

NOTES

1. University of Rochester newspaper, November 1967.

2. UPI report, 18 May 1975.

3. Aileen S. Kraditor, ed., *Up from the Pedestal* (Chicago: Quadrangle Books, 1968), p. 34.

4. Ibid., pp. 72–73.

5. Roy G. D'Andrade, "Sex Differences and Cultural Institutions," in Eleanor E. Maccoby, ed., *The Development of Sex Differences* (Stanford, Cal.: Stanford University Press, 1966) pp. 174–204.

6. Edmund S. Morgan, *The Puritan Family* (Boston, Mass.: Trustees of the Public Library, 1956).

7. Robert E. Samples, "Learning with the Whole Brain," *Human Behavior* 4 (February 1975): 16–23.

8. John Money and Anke Ehrhardt, *Man and Woman, Boy and Girl* (Baltimore: Johns Hopkins University Press, Mentor Books, 1972), p. 14.

A Christian View
of Men's and Women's Roles
in a Changing World
Part II

2

Changes in Marital Gender Roles—
Authority to Affirmation

John Scanzoni

A few years ago, the media literally bombarded Americans with the theme of family change. We heard about the generation gap, the counterculture, communes, unisex, the zany antics of some women's libbers, group marriage, and especially about the "sex revolution." The major thread connecting these various items was the notion that America was on the verge of something cataclysmic—a kind of convulsive upheaval in terms of sex and family. Many evangelists and preachers joined the chorus and prophesied that the family was decaying and in danger of collapsing. But then some funny things happened on our way to the extinction of the family. The nation's attention was turned away from these alleged catastrophes by recession, Watergate, and energy. Nevertheless an unfortunate reaction to the decrease in sensationalistic journalism could be the belief that all that "noise" about family change was a mere fad.

John Scanzoni is professor of sociology at Indiana University, where he has taught since 1964. He is the author of six books, including *Men, Women, and Change: A Sociology of Marriage and Family* which he coauthored with his wife Letha, and has contributed articles to a number of other books as well as numerous magazines.

Indeed, some have concluded that whatever was going on was ephemeral and transitory and that it's back to "business as usual" for the family.

Such a reaction is terribly unfortunate because it masks the really fundamental changes that actually are taking place. It fails to distinguish what was faddish and inconsequential from changes that are firm and of lasting significance. What is happening is at least as old as Plato's *Republic*. We find seeds of it in the New Testament and even at times in the Old Testament. Roman law supported it, and over the last four hundred years it has become pervasive throughout all modern nations. And since 1900 it has moved with considerable rapidity, especially with regard to family. We refer to a very simple yet profound notion—*individual* affirmation and all that implies.

You recall that Plato said that the state should go into all its homes to identify intelligent and gifted boys and girls from all social classes. These talented children would be trained by the state to the fullest extent of their capabilities. They would then serve as an elite pool from which the state could draw to lead its political, economic, and educational institutions. In that way the state would be utilizing its best people in the most efficient ways to achieve the most desirable and ideal society possible. Regardless of the merits of the scheme, note its revolutionary nature. It asserts that individuals should be affirmed in terms of their own talents and abilities, rather than being judged by things over which they have no control—sex, race, social class of the family into which they are born. Affirmation means giving individuals every opportunity to explore and develop all their talents, gifts, abilities to the full and rewarding them accordingly. The idea of affirming and rewarding individuals also implies that the society as a whole will be better off because of the maximum contribution of talented individuals.

Now I don't know if St. Paul ever read Plato or not; probably he did. Likewise he was probably familiar with the sentiments behind a prayer that devout Jewish males uttered each morning:

> Blessed art Thou, O Lord our God, King of the Universe,
> Who has not made me a heathen, a slave, or a woman.

Such a statement of course is the precise opposite of individual affirmation. Persons are downgraded if they happen to be members of a different racial or ethnic group (Gentiles), or of a lower economic group (slaves), or a member of the female sex (women). And worse, this prayer assumes that people are locked in to their inferior positions because of divine will and sovereignty. Thus when St. Paul wrote his first letter, Galatians, one of the most exciting parts of it is his affirmation of the individual: "There is neither Jew nor Greek, there is neither slave nor free, there is neither male nor female, for you all are one in Christ Jesus" (Gal. 3:28, RSV).

With these words, Paul takes a broadside against the ancient Jewish prayer asserting special privilege for Jews, freepersons, and men. In the context of this verse Paul is arguing that old customs and ideas have been replaced by Jesus Christ. He becomes our salvation—our life. His kingdom destroys special privilege. Within his visible church— the kingdom here and now—people of all racial and ethnic groups have equal opportunity to use all their God-given talents. The same holds for people of different socioeconomic backgrounds; and it holds just as strongly for women. What matters is not something over which the individual has no control—background factors—but rather that his or her own talents and abilities should be affirmed to the full. Not only will that person be rewarded for exercise of those gifts—the church and probably the larger society too will be better off because of it.

Unfortunately, for hundreds of years the theme of individual affirmation lay dormant both in and out of the church. The Reformation and the Renaissance breathed new life into it, and all of us are familiar with Thomas Jefferson's elegant 1776 formulation of it in the Declaration of Independence: "All Men are created equal . . . they are endowed by their Creator with certain . . . Rights . . . Life, Liberty, and the Pursuit of Happiness." But perhaps fewer of us are aware that in 1848 the Seneca Falls Convention was called by women who felt that most men were unwilling to apply Jefferson's words specifically to women. And so they met—many of them committed Christians—to revise the earlier declaration, asserting that God has given talents and gifts to women and that women ought to have full opportunity to explore these talents and use them for the good of others. Indeed, this biblical perspective characterized the writings and speeches of many nineteenth-century feminists.[1]

During this period the idea that individual affirmation was meant for women as well as men began to spread, though very slowly. And at this point changes in the conjugal family (husband, wife, dependent children) became gradually observable. Today the notion of individual affirmation is much more pervasive, and its consequences for family are much more obvious. Therefore, when we try to identify the fundamental and long-term changes in the roles of husband and wives within families, we must focus on something that's been around for at least twenty-five hundred years but only recently has become significant for women. *In short, the application of individual affirmation to women has been changing the family; it is the major force changing the family right now; and it shall continue to do so for as long into the future as anybody alive can reliably project.* Therefore, if we are going to understand what's happening to the family—what genuine changes are occurring—we must do so in the context of the changing positions and roles of women, and also of men. This fundamental issue is not a fad, nor is it ephemeral or transitory. It will not go away in five or fifty years. Such changes are part of inexorable social forces that have been contained within both church and society for two millennia.

What does individual affirmation mean in husband-wife relationships? Most Christian men have traditionally found that Christian women have been only too happy to affirm and support them. The dedicated man has said, "I will not marry if singleness will be a better vehicle for God's work through me. If I marry, it shall only be to a woman who would encourage and support me in the exercise of my gifts in whatever vocation God has for me." The central focus of the man's life has been his vocation. Men have lived apart from marriage and family, but not from occupation. If they married, family needs were "fitted in" to occupational demands.

In contrast, women have been able to live apart from vocation, but stigma and sometimes suspicion have been associated with women who lived apart from marriage and family. To be as plain and practical as possible, one basic aspect of female affirmation is the desire by an increasing number of women to experience vocation. In the past it has been common for some wives to work merely to help out with pressing family expenses. They worked at non-demanding jobs, and they generally quit when financial needs became less severe. But a very radical change is beginning to occur among increasing numbers of well-educated women. They are coming to view occupation or vocation as a right or rightful opportunity which is theirs as much as it is any other person's.

In the past men have not worked *primarily* for money but because it was the *chief means* to gain respect and identity. Besides those benefits, some jobs provide a great deal of fulfillment and satisfaction. In spite of what some say about our becoming a "leisure society," we only need observe the negative consequences for men who can't work to see how central it is to their existence. Times in point are the depressions and recessions of the thirties and seventies, or men in retirement. Men out of work become painfully aware that work is more than just money.

After all, what we call the "work ethic" to a large degree has a biblical and especially theological base.[2] We say that exercising one's gifts in vocation is the prime way for all Christians to serve God in the world. Since he will reward both now and in the future, we can concentrate on doing the work—on faithful service—rather than on the material outcomes. While the saying "work is its own reward" may be trite, it contains a germ of truth in that ideally Christians' work is supposed to be intrinsically rewarding. Affirmation means that the church gladly extends this right to women in all areas, including ordination as our Holiness and Pentecostal friends have been doing for decades.

In the days ahead an increasing number of marriages will contain two persons in vocation, or two achievers, both equally serious about the tasks to which God calls them. Interestingly, the New Testament provides an example of such a marriage, though unfortunately there are not many examples from Scripture of married couples who did engage in the biblical ideal of mutually affirming one another in the exercise of gifts. But there was at least one Christian couple who took the message of Christ seriously and supported each other's gifts.

I refer, of course, to Aquila and Priscilla. They are first mentioned in Acts 18:2. In keeping with his narrative style of writing Acts, Luke does not provide us with an overabundance of details regarding the full range of relationships between Priscilla and Aquila. Therefore we need to make certain inferences from the texts cited here and those cited below from Paul's Epistles. However, these inferences are justifiable both from the immediate contexts and from basic doctrines of Scripture such as love, freedom, justice, and dignity. Statements such as those in John 10:10 and Galatians 3:28 and 5:1 reflect these basic biblical themes.

Aquila was a Jew, and most scholars agree Priscilla was a Roman—a Gentile from an upper-class family who had been well educated as many upper-class Roman women were at that time. Evidently they had both become Christians in Rome. As Christians, they may both have been outcasts from their own extended families, but they came to love each other and to marry.

In Acts 18:3, we read that Paul stayed in Corinth with *them*—not solely with Aquila. Evidently Priscilla was not relegated to the kitchen or to the local women's sewing circle while Paul and Aquila discussed theology. Why not? Well, in the first place she was probably just as bright as they were and presumably knew as much theology as they did. And second, Paul and Aquila undoubtedly recognized those gifts in her and knew that she had to be supported in those gifts by including her as an equal partner in their discussion. And third, it is likely that Priscilla wouldn't have gone to the kitchen even if they'd asked her to. She knew that she belonged with them and that any one of them could have done the cooking as well as she.

But besides intellectual and spiritual equality, all three shared their manual skill. Priscilla and Aquila had probably picked up their ability to earn a living after being disowned. The text says that all *three* of them worked at tentmaking, not just Paul and Aquila, so that all three of them affirmed one another in their manual skills as well as in their intellectual abilities.

In verse 24, we read that both *Priscilla and* Aquila took Apollos aside and straightened out his theology. It was not just Aquila; instead each mutually supported the other in the task at hand that God had given to *both* of them. Paul mentions both of them again in Romans 16:3 as *fellow-workers,* and he says they "risked their necks" for him. Apparently Aquila and Priscilla affirmed each other in danger and manual work. And Paul says in verse 4 that all Christians give thanks to *both* of them. In verse 5, we read that they had a church together—their house. Undoubtedly each of them affirmed the other in exercising the gifts of preaching, teaching, and theology. In 1 Corinthians 16:19, we find an additional reference to their mutual ministry of preaching and teaching—the church in *their* house, together. Most Christians are aware of that body of scholarship that attributes the Epistle to the Hebrews to the pen of Priscilla.[3] Whether she actually wrote it or not, no one can be certain, but that she was spiritually and theologically competent to do so is abundantly clear. She had the necessary gifts. Moreover it seems equally clear that Aquila would have been right there supporting her in the exercise of those gifts.

That last reference to Aquila is of central significance to this whole issue of family change. So far we have focused mainly on changes in the wife's role and have said little about the kinds of changes that must necessarily take place simultaneously in the husband's role. Aquila was extraordinary for his day in the way he affirmed Priscilla and in the way he apparently "gave up" claims to inherent male power that the pagan (and Jewish) societies of his day ascribed to maleness. He was extraordinary in the ways in which he was willing to sacrifice his individual privileges and prerogatives for her sake. But ultimately, I'm sure, his willingness to be a servant, as Christ was a servant, resulted in greater good for both of them as a couple than would have been the case had he tried to exercise male power. Therefore as we discuss family changes, we need to look, not only at shifts in wives' roles, but in husbands' roles as well. We need to realize that these changes not only permit greater freedom, options, and autonomy to women, they do the same for men. By way of illustration, the originator and producer of "Sesame Street" is a woman named Joan Ganz Cooney. She administers a budget of $13 million and a staff of two hundred persons. Her husband Tim is engaged *without salary* as the head of a volunteer project among New York City blacks to train them in the use of political pressure to obtain better housing. Tim jokingly refers to himself as being like "the wife who does volunteer work."[4]

The implications of this kind of freedom—of this option —are enormous for Christians. Salaries are not available for many important tasks in the Christian community. Some married men might have gifts to perform those tasks. Their wives might have gifts which at that point in time lead them into paying jobs. It makes great sense for the sake of the kingdom of Christ for those men to perform those non-paying tasks and for their wives to be responsible for the material well-being of the family.

By the same token, many Christian wives feel restricted from the kinds of *full-time* commitment to *voluntary* work in the church or in organizations where they feel they can use their gifts for God's glory. *We must not assume that changes in the affirmation and authority of married women mean that all will seek paid employment.* Some women will use their gifts in *significant* ways as nonpaid leaders in religious, political, or community organizations. In the past many husbands have "allowed" their wives certain voluntary involvements so long as the involvements did not "interfere" with the husband's interests or plans—whether in job, family, or leisure. But affirmation of women means that if their gifts are appropriate, and if they feel so led, they should be able to participate in nonpaid tasks with the same degree of involvement and concentration that a person might give to his or her job. Obviously I'm not talking about the usual stereotypes of the ladies aid, or women's missionary and sewing circles, or weekly reviews of missionary biographies. Instead I have in mind projects within the Christian community or the larger society that are of the same order of significance as the one in which Tim Cooney is involved.

Within the family that is emerging among a steadily increasing minority of persons, the watchwords are *freedom* for the exercise of gifts and *flexibility* to allow for changes over time. At point 1, a Christian couple may both be involved in paid employment; at point 2 perhaps only the husband works while the wife uses her gifts in a nonpaying challenge; at point 3 the wife seeks paid employment while the husband pursues nonpaying challenges. These nonpaying full-time challenges could sometimes include major responsibility for childcare. Childcare could be the chief province of one parent at one point in time and of the other parent at a different point.[5]

Of course, these changes won't affect all women. Some will always prefer traditional patterns of marriage, and if that is their conviction, they must be allowed that freedom. Nevertheless, a major complaint by modern critics of marriage is that after a few years it becomes a drag—it gets old and stale, and people get tired of each other. Some married persons then get involved sexually with other equally bored married persons, and they may or may not stay married. Some couples join swingers' clubs to relieve the tedium. If they stay married, they may simply live a life of "quiet desperation." These kinds of situations are just as common in the church as out of it, but surely after five years Christian marriage should be something more than bland existence. Why do many Christian marriages suffer this malady?

There are obviously many reasons, but consider what happens to men and women when they marry. A man's life doesn't change very much; he usually keeps right on growing and developing, both personally and professionally. But when a woman marries, she experiences the first major change in her life. When a child comes along, she experiences a radical change in her personal existence. Somehow she ceases to be a person and becomes more an extension of her husband and children. While husbands develop in response to the world around them, wives turn inward to their families, forget the world, and stop developing as individuals. **1960944**

Can you imagine Priscilla, Phoebe, Lydia, Euodia, or Syntyche being forced into staleness just because they inherited femaleness? Little wonder that modern husbands and wives grow tired of each other after a few years. What does the wife have to contribute to her husband that is new and fresh and exciting? How can she understand the world outside the home that is so important to him? I believe that if Christian husbands and wives paid more attention from the outset of their marriage onward to the biblical principle of affirming each other's gifts, then there would be an ongoing, lifelong mutual stimulation of all that God put into both of them. Their marriages would be healthier, the church would be more dynamic, and the woman would retain her personhood, her unique identity in terms of what she alone can contribute as an individual to the kingdom of Christ.

Such husbands and wives are less likely to grow tired of each other; too much would be happening all the time for boredom to set in. Can you imagine Aquila and Priscilla getting tired of each other? Who knows what adventure God might next send their way? At one point, God might lead Aquila along a certain path, and Priscilla would follow. But at another point, God might lead Priscilla along a different route, and this time Aquila would follow because he loved his wife and wanted to see the exciting things God would do with her gifts.

It goes without saying that such profound changes bring challenges. Some Christians believe that these changes and challenges are evidence of decay and decline in the American family. Indeed some argue that changes are *unscriptural*. Their logic proceeds something like this: "Things are bad now in modern families, and they're getting worse. The way to reverse that trend is to go back to something we had when things were better—when families were better off." And what was that? "Greater recognition of male headship and authority." It is alleged that if men rule their households and wives are subject to them, this pleases God and makes for healthier families and persons.

If couples experience marital difficulties, they are counseled to let the husband lead and the wife follow, thus insuring a happier, more successful marriage. In recent years a new variation on this theme has emerged. Wives are advised to use sex to manipulate their husbands in subtle or covert fashion. This female, we are told, is the "fascinating woman" or the "total woman." At the same time Joe Bayly in the March 1975 issue of *Eternity* magazine reminds us that not all Christians agree as to how far male headship should be pressed. He says that while he accepts male headship he does *not* believe (in contrast to Bill Gothard and his disciples) that the Bible teaches that the father is a hammer, the wife a chisel, and the child a stone. He does not believe that the hammer is supposed to hit the chisel or that the Bible teaches any chain-of-command notion between husband and wife.

What counsel does Bayly offer Christian couples? In effect, he says, I am an executive, and I have good people working for me, yet often I let them provide input and make decisions. The result is that we are all better off because I am that kind of enlightened leader. And that, he says, is how we should counsel Christian husbands to lead their wives.

But what Bayly forgot was that he didn't get to be an executive because he is male; he got the job because he is capable. Second, he is accountable to his superiors. If Bayly's leadership and ultimate final authority lead to poor decisions that result in falling sales of his product—Sunday school materials—then Bayly's superiors will have to replace him with someone who can make better decisions.

And that is precisely the fatal flaw in the arguments of those who propose that a major solution to marital problems is some sort of ultimate male headship. There is no other social relationship in which persons or groups who hold power are not accountable to other persons or groups. The pope is accountable to cardinals; presidents are accountable to Congress and the courts; clergy are accountable to their own congregations or the presbyteries or bishops or other superiors or peers. Power must always be tempered by justice or else it corrupts, and the Nixon administration was a prime example of that.[6]

Who is to hold the husband accountable if not his wife? Who else can resist him when he is wrong? It is folly to assert "he is responsible to God." Bitter experience has convinced us of what theologians call "total depravity." Kings and clergy and presidents with unchecked power become greedy and selfish and exploit others. The same is true of husbands. The most significant point a Christian counselor can make to married couples or to those thinking about marriage is that all of this fuss, emphasis, and worry about ultimate male power can be terribly damaging to husbands and wives as persons and to the marital relationship itself. The desire to have and maintain power for its own sake can have serious negative consequences for spiritual life.

For example, you recall that the mother of James and John came to Jesus and asked that her sons be prime ministers with him after he overthrew the Roman rule of the Jews. When the remaining ten disciples heard it, they were indignant because they too wanted that power. And so Jesus said to all twelve: *"It shall not be so among you;* but whoever would be great among you must be your servant, and whoever would be first among you must be your slave; even as the Son of man came not to be served but to serve, and to give his life as a ransom for many" (Matt. 20:26–28, RSV, italics mine).

Jesus was warning about power and about its ability to corrupt. Authority or leadership for the Christian means service; it means doing what Jesus did—*giving up* rights, privileges, and power. It often means being willing to give up what one thinks is the right thing to do and letting the other person decide what is the right thing to do. And that is an extremely important point to communicate to married persons who are struggling to work out a fair and just arrangement. If each partner is occupied with letting the other person decide what is right and just, the relationship will turn out to be enormously satisfying and beneficial to both. Jesus described that strategy in very practical terms when he said, "Do for others just what you would want them to do for you" (Luke 6:31, TEV). Or to be just as practical, St. Paul said, "Let each of you look not only to his own interests, but also to the interests of others" (Phil. 2:4, RSV).

When my wife and I travel about speaking on themes of changes in men's and women's roles, the first issue that Christians raise is the theme of authority. Many Christians —especially men—are just like the disciples. They worry about power and authority when the biblical message is affirmation. The issue that the Christian man must face in terms of a Christian woman is not, How much authority do I have over you? but, What can we do for each other? What can I do *for* you?

For nineteen hundred years Christian women have not

been affirmed in terms of their gifts in the senses we described earlier. Therefore, as the servants of women, men have a special responsibility to be conscious of and to atone for the sins of their fathers. This affirmation should flow toward at least two categories of women.

First, how can the man who is married affirm his own wife? Here Aquila's behavior is our model. We may assume that he went out of his way to do four things for Priscilla. One, he consciously identified her gifts; two, he told her about them; three, he encouraged her to use them at every opportunity; four, he was willing to sacrifice some of his own interests so that she could fulfill hers. And those four things are precisely what we must encourage Christian husbands to do for their wives. The last—sacrifice of self-interest—is obviously the most difficult. Suppose, for example, a man stimulates a gift in his wife and after several years she becomes so involved in its exercise that he has to become equally or even more involved than she in childcare or domestic duties. Will he sacrifice some of his interests to take on more of those duties? Suppose an opportunity arises for her to use her gifts in another city. Would he be willing to move and leave his job in order to accommodate her interests? These are some nitty-gritty implications of Jesus' Golden Rule or Paul's words about the interests of others.

The great majority of Christian men simply do not realize that most Christian women—especially over age thirty—have not been trained to seek marital justice. All their lives they learned that it is wrong to seek justice. They learned only to serve their husbands. They often feel intense guilt if they even entertain the thought of bringing justice into balance with service. Therefore the Christian husband who seeks to affirm his wife must deal specifically with that issue of false guilt. He must remove the guilt by assuring her that it does not displease God for her to be "all she can be."[7]

Quite the contrary—it pleases God when she as a Christian woman seeks to discover and develop all her gifts and use them for his kingdom on earth.

The second category of women that men have a responsibility to affirm includes their daughters and indeed all female children ranging from pre- and actual adolescents to post-high-school women. We must rethink our whole concept of the learning or socialization of females. In the past we pointed them chiefly to role models such as Mary the mother of Jesus or Susannah the mother of John Wesley. Always it was toward being the mother of *somebody*. Their life was to be wrapped up in that of a male child; they were to be the "hand that ruled the world by rocking the cradle." But we make a serious error when we hold that up as the only or chief role model for young women to follow, for Mary the sister of Martha and Lazarus pleased Christ by discussing theology with him. The Gospels refer to wealthy women who followed Jesus and supported him and the disciples. In the Book of Acts, we read about Lydia, the businesswoman who took care of Paul and Silas at Philippi. Priscilla herself is an ideal role model for women to follow. Phoebe and Eunice and a number of others mentioned in Acts were enjoying the freedom that the Roman Empire at that particular point in time allowed a small handful of educated, highly privileged women. Down through church history, there have been other women who can serve as role models for Christian women.[8] Where would the modern missionary movement be without women such as Mary Slessor in West Africa or Gladys Aylward in China?

The point of these role models is that young Christian women should grow up learning that they have gifts of leadership or that they can contribute in many significant ways to the Christian community. In the past such contributions have been stifled, much as Archie Bunker tells Edith to "stifle yourself." Christians need to stress that *both* parents should socialize girls in this way. At the same time it is very important that younger boys be trained to respect females, not as *feminine dolls* or fragile ladies, but as equal persons who can contribute just as much as they in all areas of life.

Unfortunately many Christians worry about authority and forget about affirmation. Some worry that the Bible teaches that woman's place is to recognize man's *headship*, that somehow God made men and women different in more than anatomy. Unfortunately, we have space only to begin to probe this issue.[9] Earlier I pointed out that those who hold power must also be held accountable. Only God—omnipotent and omniscient—is accountable to no human being. All humans including husbands must be held accountable to other humans. But how does one interpret Paul's admonition for wives to be "subject" to husbands? Many of us have talked to persons who struggle with those words in light of Paul's saying that all Christians should be "subject to each other" (Eph. 5:21) or that male-female distinctions in privilege and power are no more (Gal. 3:28). What do we say to persons who are puzzled by this seeming inconsistency? [10]

First, Paul was writing to a pagan world in which wives were already subordinate to their husbands. Why should he tell them to do something they were already doing? The only answer that makes sense is that some Christian women had taken his earlier statement in Galatians seriously and were agitating for freedom and equality. The sad fact is that the vast majority of those women were not ready for freedom. They were ignorant and illiterate, and their husbands kept them that way—barefoot, pregnant, and in the kitchen. Furthermore, there would have been no place for them in the larger Roman society. That kind of revolution—

or a similar rumbling by Christian slaves—would have brought persecutions from Rome even more severe than they already faced.

Therefore, Paul, in order to preserve *order*, tells Christian wives to keep on being subordinate, but he adds, "as to the Lord." He takes the sting out of what they know to be unfair by saying "do it for Jesus' sake, and for the sake of order in the kingdom." Then he tells husbands to love their wives as much as "Christ loved the church" or as much as "they love themselves." That kind of love or headship means servanthood in which rights and privileges are given up for the good of the other.

But recall that tiny percentage of educated women such as Priscilla, Phoebe, Euodia, and Syntyche? Paul didn't have these dear friends and co-workers in mind when he wrote about continued subjection. These women were every bit the equals of their husbands in the home and out of it. And what of today? More and more Christian women are getting more and more education. They are waiting to be affirmed so that they can contribute to the kingdom. To dwell on the authority question in a selfish manner is to sidetrack the important practical questions of how to affirm women in today's changing world!

The inevitable changes in men's and women's roles and the changes in marriage and family can be beneficial, healthy and good. We need a vision to see what new and exciting things women can contribute to men, to the church, to marriage, to other women. We need a vision to see how women can contribute to their own well-being as persons—as Christian disciples. Once we catch sight of how exciting and challenging and interesting it would be if women were affirmed, we would begin to do it with considerable enthusiasm.

Doing it raises many practical questions for the Christian, some of which we've already mentioned. But once we catch a vision of "all that women can be" and all that marriage can be once women are affirmed, then the Christian can begin to grapple successfully with the practical problems.

NOTES

1. Letha Scanzoni, "The Feminists and the Bible," *Christianity Today*, 2 February 1973, pp. 10–15.

2. John Scanzoni, "The Christian View of Work," in C. F. H. Henry, ed., *Quest for Reality: Christianity and the Counter Culture* (Downers Grove, Ill.: Inter-Varsity Press, 1973), pp. 89–101.

3. Letha Scanzoni and Nancy Hardesty, *All We're Meant to Be* (Waco, Tex.: Word Books, 1974), p. 217.

4. Shephard G. Aronson, "Marriage with a Successful Woman: A Personal Viewpoint," *Annals of the New York Academy of Sciences*, 15 March 1973, pp. 218–26.

5. Space does not permit me to delve into the issue of children during this period of change. However, I have explored it in detail in "Rethinking Christian Perspectives on Family Planning and Population Control," *Calvin College Symposium*, October 1975.

6. John Scanzoni, "Authority in Christian Marriage," *Reformed Journal*, November 1975, pp. 20–24.

7. Scanzoni and Hardesty, *All We're Meant to Be.*

8. See Nancy Hardesty's series "Great Women of Faith" over several months in 1974–75 *Eternity* magazine.

9. See J. Scanzoni, "Authority in Marriage," for a fuller treatment of the authority question.

10. See Scanzoni and Hardesty, *All We're Meant to Be,* for a fuller treatment.

3

Femininity Today:
Walking the Knife-Edge

Mary Stewart Van Leeuwen

Christian women in North America hover uncertainly under the bombardment of two apparently opposite messages. Each is plausibly and vociferously defended by its share of Christian scholars, exegetes, pastors, lay persons, and social scientists. One camp insists that (read correctly) Scripture, history, biology, and psychology all combine to affirm that women are primarily to be domestic creatures, living vicariously through service to the family and most fulfilled in a submissive, protected relationship with fathers, husbands, and male church leaders. I could spend much time cataloguing the representatives, past and present, of this point of view, but since many other writers of recent books and articles have taken on this task,[1] I will content you with only a couple of brief examples. John Milton, whose distinctively Christian world-view did much to convince the stubbornly atheistic C. S. Lewis of God's claims on his life, clearly saw man under God and woman under man in a

Mary Stewart Van Leeuwen is assistant professor of psychology, York University, Toronto, Canada. She holds a B.A. degree from Queen's University, Kingston, Ontario, and M.A. and Ph.D. degrees from Northwestern University. Her many publications focus on social and crosscultural psychology as well as sex roles and sexuality.

hierarchically patterned universe. In *Paradise Lost* (Book 4), Eve addresses Adam:

> My author and disposer, what thou bidd'st
> Unargued I obey; so God ordains:
> God is thy law, thou mine: to know no more
> Is woman's happiest knowledge, and her praise.[2]

And in a manner hardly as literary, but no less convinced, Marabel Morgan (of *Total Woman* fame) insists that

> A total woman . . . graciously chooses to adapt to her husband's way, even though at times she desperately may not want to. . . . Marriage has been likened to a monarchy, where the husband is king and his wife is queen. In a royal marriage, the king's decision is the final word, for his country and his queen alike. . . . Though the king relies heavily on her judgment, if there is a difference of opinion, it is the king who makes the final decision. . . . If the king makes the wrong decision, even when the queen *knows* she's right . . . the queen is still to follow him forthwith. A queen shall not nag or buck her king's decision once it is made.[3]

In the opposite camp to such traditionalists, and speaking no less insistently and articulately, are apologists of both sexes for a thoroughgoing Christian feminism and an egalitarian view of the universe in which men and women, as equally redeemed sinners under the lordship of Christ and the empowering of the Holy Spirit, together face the derision and corruption of an apostate world and fight to establish God's kingdom of righteousness and justice.[4] Again, I could regale you with numerous examples of this position, but I want rather to present one rather striking illustration as expressed by a Catholic mother and scholar. She struggled with these issues back in the fifties when both Christianity and feminism were having a very bad press (or no press at all) and when to be *both* a Christian and a feminist was unheard of.

I can honestly say that my conversion to Christianity preceded my feminism, and aided and abetted it. Without taking Christianity seriously, I would never have been prepared to accept feminism.

First and foremost, serious Christianity taught me to reappraise the world I knew with a different eye. As a Christian, I could no longer accept the passing scene with a shrug and, "Well, that's just the way things are." I became critical of everything, because I measured everything by Christ's words in the gospel and the rest of the New Testament. The value of each individual whom God loved was not to be ignored, suppressed, or harmed in any way. . . .

I also got the very clear message that the responsibility for bringing the Kingdom of God to earth was mine. No excuse of weakness or anything else was accepted. It never occurred to me that because I was a woman I could excuse myself from the tasks to be done. After all, there were the woman saints to look to; and since God worked through weakness (according to Saint Paul), what did it matter that I didn't belong to the dominant caste, or sex? My aspiration was to serve and love and change the world, and femininity didn't seem to be something that would get in the way. . . .

In secular society during the '50's, especially in intellectual academic circles, Christianity was considered an unacceptable ideology. One got used to being considered "queer," "odd," "different," "fanatic," and so on. I learned early the effort to go against the crowd, even those I most admired, and stick to my unpopular beliefs.

I was also saved from (a related temptation), that in which women aim only to please others, particularly if they are men. In serious Christianity, the point was to get beyond appearances and the desire to exercise power over others. As a woman, I wanted to look nice, but pleasing men was not as important as pleasing God by right actions. . . . Depth of personality and intelligence were more valuable than popularity. . . . Christianity forced me to give up my female narcissism, as much as I could manage, anyway. My aim was to make something of myself, not to make it with men.[5]

So here we have what seem to be two fundamentally incompatible positions regarding femininity, or womanhood, each insisting that the weight of Scripture, history, science, and common sense is on its side. The one insists that godly womanhood is to be realized primarily in the context of service and obedience in a specific family and community context. The other avers that true Christianity calls women beyond the confines of traditional roles to bold, innovative, and seemingly unrestricted areas of service for the kingdom. Which is right?

There is some solid basis for *each* of these views in Scripture. In the Genesis account, Eve is created after Adam and as his helpmeet; yet God holds them *both* equally responsible for the sin into which they fall. Later, in the early church, a similar ambivalence prevails. Male leaders are clearly in the majority; yet Ananias and Sapphira bear equal responsibility and equal punishment for attempting to deceive God and their fellows in the sale of their property (Acts 5). The virtuous wife of Proverbs 31 is obviously an astute and independent businesswoman as well as a concerned homemaker. Paul tells his constituency that wives are to be subject to their husbands and restrained in their participation in services; yet frequently he commends the work of women deacons in the same breath as he praises the men. Elsewhere he maintains (Gal. 3:28) that in Christ the barriers of race, class, and sex are broken down. Christ chooses an inner circle of men as disciples; yet he so upsets the status quo in his egalitarian treatment of women that even the disciples find it hard to take (John 4). We could multiply such examples indefinitely, but I think you see my point— *both* the hierarchical and the egalitarian view of women find support in Scripture. One has merely to select judiciously and argue cleverly in order to make an almost watertight case for either point of view.

Now, if I were writing primarily as a theologian and an exegete, I would say that the basic issue is clearly hermeneutical. It includes such questions as how we determine the *nature* and *purpose* of Scripture; the extent to which we look to scriptural *details* or underlying *principles* for guidance; on what basis we decide *which texts* are the determining ones, and whether certain scriptural injunctions are to be considered binding for all time, or for purely local application in response to specific problems, such as those which beset the young church at Corinth. But I am neither an exegete nor a theologian and must leave such questions to others for their solution—if there is one.[6] Besides, the academic issue of how we interpret Scripture is unlikely to be of immediate help to the Christian woman trying to decide *now* how to run her life in the face of these seemingly conflicting messages. The more practical issue is, How do we live with this dilemma in an almost day-by-day effort to discern the Spirit of God for our lives?

First, and most important, let us never fall into the trap of believing that the dilemma will be resolved for us theologically. It would be nice if we could simply get an equal number of equally well-trained men and women exegetes defending each point of view eventually to come up with a score card which decisively favors one over the other. Such exercises are perhaps good and necessary to jolt each of us out of a mind-set too rigidly bent one way or the other, but when it comes to making decisions about *my* particular life, God calls me to exercise obedience on the basis of *wisdom*, not logical argument. And the two are not the same. Logic (and *theo*logic) is rigid, deterministic, and admits no exceptions to its conclusions, whatever they may be. But the wisdom of the Holy Spirit is much more tailor-made; it defies and transcends the petty, manmade theological categories of any age. It calls me to steep myself in the Word as a whole, in an attitude of openness and obedience, and then to be prepared for some surprises. When God's Spirit is at work, somehow the unexpected always happens: scrawny little boys kill giants; a self-conscious stutterer becomes the architect of the nation Israel; a peasant girl becomes the mother of God incarnate; the would-be murderer of the young church becomes its chief evangelist.

I do not expect things to be much different today, and so it is no surprise when one woman friend tells me that God is calling her to renounce a brilliant professional career and be more exclusively a companion and helper to her husband. But equally, it is no surprise when another woman friend tells me that God is convicting her to leave the comfortable confines of domesticity and return to school to get a degree. It may well be that God is working out basically the same agenda in both lives. Perhaps he is doing some idol smashing in both. The one woman may have been too preoccupied with her prestigious position; the other, with her beautiful house and matchless cuisine. Both may be called to renounce the comforts of a given routine and set of rewards and strike out into uncharted territory. The professional woman who is used to dealing with people and ideas in the abstract may need to learn how God can work in concrete, quiet, one-to-one relationships, and the housewife who has hitherto believed that her *only* gifts are in concrete service to her family may be called to learn a new boldness before an expanded constituency.

Second, I think God detests mere ax-grinding for its own sake. It is one thing for me to conclude that I have too long bought the traditional female role and now need to pursue an activity in some hitherto masculine sphere; it is quite another thing for me to decide that if all my friends don't do the same, they are being brainwashed, narrow, and irresponsible Christians. It is no mark of liberation to be forced from one set of restricted options to an opposite, but equally restrictive, set. If the notion of spiritual gifts means anything, it means that I have the freedom—and the responsibility—to discover my unique place and ministry in God's scheme of things in response to *his* Word and *his* Spirit, whether that means doing something apparently traditional or something quite innovative.

Third, it is possible to do a good thing from a bad motive. In this era many Christians, for many reasons, live in reaction to their past. The person from an anti-intellectual, fundamentalist background may as a consequence decide that intellect is everything and that getting a Ph.D. will supply all the answers to life. Conversely, the person raised in an atmosphere where intellect and theologizing were overvalued may become a hypercharismatic in a valid search for the experiential dimension to his Christian life. In a similar vein, I suspect that many Christian women have been hurt by their families and churches as young people because their particular gifts and inclinations did not happen to fit the stereotyped notions of what was feminine. It is entirely understandable if, in reaction (and I am *not* saying that *all* Christian feminists react this way), they determine to out-articulate their opposition and resolutely claim their place in the ecclesiastical sun. But I cannot stress strongly enough the necessity to grow beyond this attitude, especially if there is in it any trace of bitterness or a vindictive satisfaction in "getting back" at the people who have wronged you and limited you in times past. Aside from the fact that such a spirit of bitterness is never condoned scripturally and can thwart the working of the Holy Spirit, the person living out of reaction to his or her past is not in the least *free* from that past. On the contrary, he or she is still being very much determined by it and, as a result, has categorically decided that certain options are unthinkable. To be more specific, we must be careful not to let our own *individual* negative experience of family life, for example, lead us to conclude that the *institution* is intrinsically oppressive or outdated; nor, must we let our experience with one pushy career woman lead us to conclude that females should never be in positions of authority.[7] Until each of us, male and female, is ready to deal with such emotional issues *existentially* before God as well as *theologically* in the forum of the church, the larger question of women's roles and women's place will continue to be debated totally in the realm of the flesh—and ultimately only the adversary will win.

Finally, I would stress the necessity of being aware that the choices we make as Christian women must be faced on two different levels simultaneously: the first is with reference to God's agenda for our *personal* sanctification, and the second is God's agenda for the building of the *kingdom* in the time and place he has allotted each of us in history. The first is an inward-looking, personal struggle with sin, temptation, self-acceptance, and a host of other issues known only to God, ourselves, and (if we are so fortunate) one or two trusted confidantes. The second level involves an outward-looking, activist concern for the health of the church, and ultimately the whole world, which necessarily takes us beyond our individual concerns and asks, What is to be done for the community at large? To think that we have to make our choices as women on one level or the other is false and unbiblical. If we are sincere in our desire to obey God and to follow the leading of the Holy Spirit, then our lives will be all of one piece; there will not be a false dichotomy between personal and communal aspects. We will neither be activists whose personal relationship to God has shriveled to nothing, nor will we be pietists who are so heavenly minded that we are no earthly good. We will be, instead, progressively more whole people, flexibly responsive to God's call to be light and salt by the testimony of both our personal lives and our dealings with each other and the world at large. By this criterion, the *content* of our roles is not nearly so important as the *style* and the *spirit*. One can be an outwardly obedient, traditional housewife internally seething with unvoiced resentment and rebellion; one can be a champion for women's rights in a spirit of humble obedience to God and service to the kingdom. Either way, by our fruits we shall be known: by the way we generate not divisiveness but unity; not self-aggrandizement but a spirit of humble service; not clever word-games aimed at scoring points but wisdom for a particular situation at a particular time. These are the criteria of our walk with the Spirit whether we are men or women, traditionalists or feminists, educated or uneducated, old or young. Let us not be seduced into mistaking secondary questions about the content of our roles as women for the more primary questions about our responsibilities as Christians. If we are truly attending to the latter, the former will take care of themselves.

NOTES

1. See, for example, Larry Christensen, *The Christian Family* (Minneapolis: Bethany Fellowship, 1970); Bill Gothard, *Institute for Basic Youth Conflicts* (Seminar Notes); T. Howard, "A Traditionalist View," *Post-American*, May 1975, pp. 8–15; Marabel Morgan, *The Total Woman* (Old Tappan, N.J.: Fleming H Revell, 1973); Charles C. Ryrie, *The Role of Women in the Church* (Chicago: Moody Press, 1966); and other examples cited by Letha Scanzoni and Nancy Hardesty, *All We're Meant to Be* (Waco, Tex.: Word Books, 1974).

2. John Milton, *Paradise Lost and Other Poems* (New York: New American Library, 1961).

3. Morgan, *Total Woman*, p. 71. This extract is from a chapter entitled "Adapt to Him" and a section subheaded "Oh, King, Live Forever."

4. See, for example, *Daughters of Sarah* (a Christian-feminist newsletter) (Chicago: Christian Coalition, 1974 and on); S. B. Doely, ed., *Women's Liberation and the Church* (New York: Association Press, 1970); "Evangelical Feminism," *Post-American* 3, no. 6 (1974), and articles by Thomas Howard and Donald

Dayton in *Post-American* 5, no. 4 (1975); Scanzoni and Hardesty, *All We're Meant to Be;* P. K. Jewett, *Man As Male and Female* (Grand Rapids: Eerdmans, 1975).

5. Sidney C. Callahan, "A Christian Perspective on Feminism," in Doely, *Women's Liberation and the Church.*

6. Hermeneutical and exegetical issues concerning women are treated in Donald Dayton, "An Egalitarian View," *Post-American* 4, no. 4 (1975); Krister Stendahl, *The Bible and the Role of Women* (Philadelphia: Fortress Press, 1966).

7. I am grateful to my husband Raymond C. Van Leeuwen for helping me to clarify the points made in this paragraph.

4

Masculinity Today

Gary R. Collins

> You had no choice about being a male.
> You do about being a man.
> Most of your personal happiness
> and all of your success as a human being
> depend on seeing the need to make that choice,
> and on having the courage to do it.[1]

These are the words of a Catholic priest, and they hit the
nail right on the head. Being male is easy; being masculine
is not. We had no choice about our sex. This was a matter
of genes, determined without our approval at the instant of
conception and revealed at the time of birth. On the other
hand, males do have a choice about being masculine. Parents, of course, dress boys in blue and treat male children
differently from females,[2] but in the long run, the individual
male determines for himself the extent to which he will be
masculine.

Gary R. Collins is professor of psychology at Trinity Evangelical
Divinity School, Deerfield, Illinois, and the author of several books
on psychology and counseling. He was program director for the
Continental Congress on the Family in St. Louis at which the chapters in this book were given. He and his wife Julie have two
daughters.

THE MASCULINE IMAGE

There was a time, not many years ago, when it was relatively easy to describe what it meant to be masculine. Fathers wanted their sons to be ambitious and muscular. To be truly masculine meant that one was strong, aggressive, self-confident, outgoing, and perhaps a little domineering. Interest in the outdoors and proficiency in sports contributed to the image. In addition, the really masculine male was expected to be sexually aggressive but disinclined to show emotions like tenderness, sensitivity, or compassion.

With masculinity so clearly defined, boys and men have had a standard to strive for, and each has had a guideline for judging the masculinity of another. To avoid being labeled a "sissy" or something worse, many boys have learned to fight back tears even when they felt deeply moved, to go to camp when they would have preferred the indoors, to build muscles and go out for sports when they were not athletically inclined. In neighborhoods where fathers are often unknown or not very often present, boys have formed gangs to prove their toughness and to learn aggressive masculinity from their peers. A lot of high-school and college males still try drinking, profanity, and heterosexual conquest—which sometimes ends in pregnancy and often leads to a lot of grief—in an attempt to prove their manhood.

Trying to fit the masculine image doesn't always stop when one turns twenty-one. Many males go through life trying to prove to others, but mostly to themselves, that they are really men. Sexual exploits, drinking with the boys, boasting about one's noninvolvement in housework, the making of unilateral decisions at home, showing aggressive mannerisms (often behind the wheel of a car), and hiding emotions are all attempts to appear ruggedly male. In contrast some men give up and become passive, dominated, and weak. But passive males, like their aggressive counterparts, are really failures in the quest for masculinity. They are living a never-ending struggle to prove they are really men.

Why should any male care about being considered masculine? One's self-esteem appears largely to be dependent on one's identity as a male or a female.[3] If I as a male am unable to live up to society's expectations about what it means to be a real man, I feel threatened and a failure. According to a respected marriage counselor, "One of the commonest problems confronted by persons who do marriage counseling is dealing with men who secretly harbor fears that they are not men. . . . A husband may be sure he is a male, but highly uncertain as to whether he has acquired those attributes which he considers masculine. This uncertainty opens Pandora's box to a whole host of problems in husband-wife relationships."[4] It also creates problems concerning one's self-esteem, success in life, and inner security.

This struggle to fit a stereotyped masculine image creates numerous problems. Masculinity, as presently conceived in the popular mind, is unhealthy, unrealistic, rapidly changing, and psychologically harmful.

Several years ago, a psychologist at the University of Florida wrote a paper suggesting that the male role in our society is not only harmful but "lethal."[5] If a man equates masculinity with being tough, aggressive, unsentimental, businesslike, emotionally unexpressive, and always striving to get ahead, then he has no alternative but to suppress his personal needs, feelings, and insecurities. This takes effort, consumes energy, and puts the body under stress. As a result the male is more susceptible to ulcers, heart attacks, strokes, and premature death. As long as men can only see themselves as being manly when they are pushing to get ahead, sexually potent, and physically virile, then they are basing their whole lives on a tenuous and potentially destructive foundation. Instead of a slavish adherence to the traditional but lethal definition of masculinity, this Florida psychologist advocated self-disclosure—honestly sharing with others our hopes and hurts, even when such openness doesn't fit the stereotype of what is masculine.

A second problem with the traditional image of masculinity is that almost nobody fits. Deep inside men know that they often are sensitive, passive, gentle, insecure, and needing to depend on others—the very antithesis of the popular definition of masculinity. Some males simply do not have athletic abilities or bulging muscles (except around the stomach). They want the freedom to express love openly and even to cry (as Jesus did). They have no desire to be tough, aggressive, or ruthless in their careers, and they are not inclined to jump into bed with women other than their wives. Nevertheless, for many males, life is a struggle to be something they aren't, to attain an image of masculinity which is unattainable. This playboy or cowboy image,[6] if it ever is attained, does not make a real male but rather an insecure nonadult who plays a phony role instead of relaxing and learning to be his authentic self.

Within recent years, however, this traditional definition of masculinity has begun to crumble. Male physical strength is no longer needed or valued in our society. As women have shown that they can be independent, athletic, responsible, intellectually capable, strong, sexually aggressive, and effective in the business world, men have discovered that they no longer have automatic status, higher pay, and opportunity solely because of their sex. Now men can't even maintain their identity by dressing uniquely. Women wear pantsuits, and male styles are becoming increasingly colorful, frilly, and (frankly) feminine. Men can laugh about these changes, ignore them, or even try to resist them, but as the woman's place in society changes, so does the man's. Men are being forced to deal with a new definition of masculinity which already is influencing the family and family living.

As traditional male roles blur, many men face what one writer calls "the male dilemma."[7] John Wayne and Hugh Heffner no longer epitomize masculinity in America, and with the old models gone, males (when they allow themselves to think about it) are confused. They are looking for a new definition of masculinity and a new way to prove to themselves and the world that they are male.

According to Wallace Denton[8] males react in several ways to this dilemma. Some develop a *domineering* attitude and turn to authoritarian mannerisms as a way of asserting masculinity. They bolster their inner weaknesses by bossing others around—especially women. At home and at work they become tyrants, making demands of others and giving frequent reminders of who is in charge. While pushing others around, they fail to realize that real men who know they are men have no need to continuously remind their families and themselves that they are the head of the home.

A second reaction to the male dilemma is *dependency*, the exact antithesis of dominance. Dependent men show little ambition and may drift from job to job. They rely on a domineering or otherwise more capable wife, leave the bills and child discipline for their spouses to handle, and sometimes are clearly henpecked. Men who abdicate the headship in a home often turn to alcohol or gambling in an attempt to hide their inadequacy and reassure others (but especially themselves) that they are really men—doing manly things like going out on the town with the boys.

Sexual problems present a third type of reaction to the male dilemma. Some men lose interest in sex and become impotent, perhaps unconsciously expressing hostility toward women. Some go in the opposite direction and, while really showing an equal contempt for women, engage in sexual exploits—at home or away—trying to prove their manhood or ability to perform as males.

Pseudomasculinity is the fourth unhealthy reaction to the male dilemma. According to Denton:

> The pseudomasculine man looks and behaves so much according to traditional concepts of masculinity that no one would ever suspect that harbored within are conscious or unconscious fears about being unmasculine. But they are there. This man may be a big, double-jointed football player who looks anything but feminine. He may be a weight lifter, be preoccupied with his physique and the muscles that ripple over his well-developed body. This hairy-chested, but uncertain, man may delight in engaging in dangerous occupations or activities such as auto racing and high structural steel work.[9]

Of course, not all muscular, sports-loving men are attempting to prove their manhood, but some, in order to hide their fear of being unmasculine, develop a ruggedly masculine mode of life.

Some men presumably ignore the male dilemma, assuming that the uncertainty, like women's lib, will pass with the next generation of hair styles. Some resist the change, fighting vainly to keep women in their "proper place" and ignoring the legitimate demands of women for equal rights, equal pay, equal opportunities, and equal work. Perhaps the majority of men acknowledge that change is inevitable and try, without giving it a lot of thought, to find some comfortable midpoint between the old male chauvinist roles and the demands of the most vocal "women's libbers."

One of the most popular answers to the male-female identity problem suggests that we forget sex roles altogether and just "be the individual people we were meant to be."

There has been talk of the not-too-distant day when men and women will share the same public washroom facilities, wear identical clothing, play on the same ball teams, compete for the same jobs, fight alongside each other in wars, and share household responsibilities equally, while babies are produced in test tubes and developed scientifically in artificial uteri. One writer, however, has argued persuasively that this would not only bring "sexual suicide" but a disintegration of society itself.[10] As is widely known, this unisex idea was tried following the 1917 Revolution in the Soviet Union, but it didn't work, and a greater differentiation of roles was soon reintroduced.[11] Following his review of the psychiatric and psychological literature, E. M. Pattison concluded that although our definitions of maleness and femaleness are certain to keep changing in the future, "we cannot and should not eradicate a definite sense of maleness and femaleness." A clearly defined male and female sexual identity is critically important, Pattison argues, if we are to maintain a sense of self-identity. We cannot answer the question, Who am I? without making some reference to our maleness or femaleness.

Such a conclusion would appear consistent with the Scriptures. While it is true that both sexes are equal in the sight of God and we are all one in Christ Jesus, it is also clear that God made us two sexes. He must have had some purpose in doing so, and proof rests with the advocates of unisex to show that God intended sexual differences to be obliterated.

THE MASCULINE IDENTITY

The old masculine image is going or gone, and that's probably good. But as a new definition of maleness is evolving, men are striving without any clear standard of masculinity against which to test their efforts.

How then do we define masculinity today? Do we let in-

dividual males—including young developing males—floun-
der to find their own sexual and self-identity, or can there
be guidelines to male identity even in this age of evolving
standards?

In Proverbs 31 we read a vivid description of what the
ideal female is like, but the Scriptures give no parallel picture of the truly masculine male. There are numerous por-
traits of real men in the Bible, however, and guidelines for
fathers and husbands. From these references we can piece
together a picture of masculinity which leaves room for individual differences and cultural changes but which also
gives stable guidelines for the male who would be truly
masculine.[13]

*First, to be truly masculine is to be a follower and imitator
of Jesus Christ.* Christ was the only perfect man who ever
lived, and his life is a model for males today (1 Pet. 2:21).
Space does not permit a complete description of the manli-
ness of Jesus, but some characteristics come to mind immediately. He was:

—dependent on God for daily guidance, frequently at
  prayer, and thoroughly familiar with the Scriptures;
—morally upright, absolutely intolerant of sin, and a firm
  defender of justice;
—compassionate, sensitive to the needs of others, and not
  afraid to show his feelings;
—knowledgeable of events and situations around him,
  concerned about the poor and needy, actively involved
  in alleviating suffering, sincerely interested in people,
  and willing to tolerate individual personality differences
  in others;
—a perfect model of the Spirit-filled life-style in that his
  whole being was characterized by love, joy, peace,
  patience, kindness, goodness, faithfulness, gentleness,
  and self-control.

This presents a very high standard, but it is clearly defined, and males can reach it when they commit their lives to Jesus Christ, deliberately avoid sin, and seek the daily guidance of the Holy Spirit. Cultural definitions of masculinity change over the years and from place to place; the standard we have in Christ remains firm both today and forever.

Second, true masculinity consists of overtly resisting the devil and growing as a man of God. This is the exact opposite of the popular masculine image. Males in our society often assert their masculinity by engaging in aggressive and sexually immoral behavior, but the Bible describes this as sinful and ultimately self-defeating. In addition, many modern men seem to view religion as a crutch for the emotionally unstable, an escape from reality which self-sufficient men do not need.

The early disciples did not reflect this view. They were sensitive but bold men who were involved in successful vocations before risking their health, status, comfort, and lives for the cause of Christ. They were decisive men who knew what they believed, could defend their faith intellectually, refused to cower in the face of opposition, had a clear purpose for living, squarely faced the issue of life after death, were bold enough to proclaim what they believed in spite of certain opposition, treated both women and men with respect, and were honest enough to acknowledge that their sinful lives needed the help and molding influence that comes from a loving Savior and Lord. The truly masculine man avoids sinful behavior, admits both his weaknesses and his need for divine guidance, and does not try to cover his insecurities with noisy exhibitions of independence, strength, or virility.

Third, the truly masculine male recognizes and accepts his unique abilities and weaknesses. Popular images of masculinity set up standards which nobody can reach and which are confusing because they are always changing. Why should a sensitive man hide his feelings of love, tenderness, or compassion just because this isn't supposed to be masculine? Why should a nonathlete force himself into doing something which he hates just because real men are supposed to be "jocks"? Why should we encourage young boys to flirt with girls, pretend to be tough, or squelch their interest in classical music to fit somebody's fleeting definition of masculinity?

This attitude has created much confusion among women who are trying to be feminine. Betty Freidan, Marabel Morgan, Germaine Greer, and a host of lesser known women have carved out their personal views of femininity and appear to try forcing all women to fit. The same thing could happen to the male quest for masculinity. We could have a myriad of voices trying to push every insecure male into some kind of a mold which is supposed to represent true masculinity.

It is far more honest and desirable for individual males (and females) to acknowledge openly their strengths and weaknesses, to confess their sins, to give up on trying to succeed in areas where they are naturally incapable, to develop their unique gifts or abilities, and to recognize that God has made each of us different. In an attempt to be all he is meant to be, the masculine male does not struggle to conform to some image. He recognizes his uniquenesses and is bold enough to be himself—an authentic, honest human being.

Fourth, true masculinity involves the freedom to acknowledge one's sexuality. When God made us male and female, he was not advocating unisex. Apparently he wanted the sexes to be different. He knew about hormones, sexual temptations, the ease with which men can get "turned on" sexually, and the struggles many men have in keeping their sexual urges under control. He created sex, not only for reproduction, but for enjoyment and need fulfillment. In the Bible, sex within marriage is called honorable (Heb. 13:4). The enjoyment that a man can have in bed with a woman is described with approval and in vivid detail (Song of Sol.). In a discussion of personal holiness the writer of 1 Corinthians (6:19–7:5) feels comfortable in freely discussing sexual intercourse.

As every male knows, sex can be misused and control is sometimes difficult, but this is no reason to deny that we are sexual creatures. God made us this way, and we should be grateful both for the construction of our male bodies and for the sexual urges that cause these bodies to react erotically. Males must be alert to the dangers of uncontrolled sex, to the ease with which sex can be misused, to the power of the Holy Spirit in helping men to control and channel their sexual urges, and to the exceptional physical intimacy that is possible through sex within marriage.

Fifth, the truly masculine male is sensitive to the needs of women and alert to his responsibilities as husband and father. The playboy and cowboy images of masculinity consider women as objects to be used, manipulated, and enjoyed but rarely respected. In contrast, the Bible gives women a place of importance equal with men (Gal. 3:23). They are described as physically the "weaker sex" (1 Pet. 3:7, rsv), but are to be accorded honor, respect, understanding, and sensitivity. Undoubtedly this involves treating women as human beings who have needs, feelings, capabilities, intelligence, and both the ability and desire to do more creative things than changing diapers or washing socks.

Within marriage the husband has three major responsibilities in the home. He must take responsibility for leadership of the family; he must provide for his wife's needs; and he must love his wife (1) as Christ loved the church, (2) as men love their own bodies, and (3) as men love themselves. To reach this biblical standard of masculinity within marriage husbands are not commanded to beat their wives into submission or to lecture about male authority in the home. According to one writer the task is a lot different.[14] First, the husband must give up his own rights for the sake of his wife. This, of course, is what Jesus did for us, and he is the model for us to follow in marriage (Eph. 5:25). Second, the husband takes care of his wife just as he cares for his own body (Eph. 5:28, 33). The Golden Rule then applies in marriage as the husband treats his wife as he wants her to treat him. Third, the husband helps his wife to reach her goals just as he seeks to reach his. Within marriage there is a hierarchy of responsibility (Eph. 5:22–24), but there is a mutual respect (Eph. 5:33) and even a submission one to another (Eph. 5:21). Such a pattern, if diligently followed, would eliminate henpecked husbands, domineering wives, and men who try to achieve masculinity by being tough at home.

For a man to criticize, stifle, or put down a woman is not a mark of masculinity. It is an expression of insensitivity and immaturity. It shows a male ego being threatened and a failure to realize that women who are given love, respect, and security very often respond with support, cooperation, and love.

With this kind of marriage relationship a man is prepared to be a good father. According to the Scriptures men are not free to leave the disciplining and parenting roles to the mother although she has a vitally important role in child-rearing. As recorded in the Bible, men are to:

—obey the Word of God so they can bring up their children properly (Deut. 6:1–2);
—love their children and express this both verbally and

by actions so that the young people are not exasperated because of harsh, insensitive criticism (Deut. 6:5; Col. 3:21);

—discipline their children in order to correct misbehavior (Eph. 6:4);

—provide for the physical and social needs of children (2 Cor. 12:14).

It is not necessary for a man to be a husband and father to be masculine. Jesus never married, and Paul argued that a single man could serve God in a special way because there was no wife or family to distract from the Lord's work (1 Cor. 7:32–35). If a male marries and has children, however, he is not truly masculine until he conforms to the biblical guidelines for husbands and fathers. Whether he is a family man or not, the real man treats all women and children with the respect they deserve.

MASCULINE FAMILY LIFE

These five guidelines for masculinity have a great relevance for the family today. Many current problems in the home can be traced to a failure of men to live up to these principles. When men ignore Jesus Christ, they have at best a changing standard for masculinity, and often they are more concerned about asserting their personal conception of maleness than growing as men of God, secure in their relationship with Christ. When men fail to acknowledge their weaknesses as well as their strengths, they are so busy trying to fit some image that they often are insensitive to the needs of wives or children and more concerned about asserting their ego-centered superiority over others. When men fail to acknowledge sex as a gift from God, they use sex to dominate or abuse women and to prove to themselves that they really are male. When men ignore the biblical guidelines for marriage and the family, they are left in a state of confusion, uncertain about how to run their homes. In the lower socioeconomic and ghetto areas, such men often disappear, leaving childrearing responsibilities to the wife and leaving the children to work out their own definitions of masculinity and maturity. In the suburbs, the man often remains at home but withdraws emotionally—sometimes even to an overinvolvement in Christian activities. The wife is left to make the decisions and raise the family because the father has given up his responsibilities. Little wonder that frustrated and overworked wives take over in the home. They have no alternative. The abdication of men from leadership in the home is in my opinion one of the major causes for family problems in America today.

The time has come for males to rise up again, to conform to the image of masculinity based on the Scriptures, to reassume a loving, considerate leadership in the home, and to be the men God meant them to be. The real solution to marriage and family problems may very well begin with a changed attitude in men who have forsaken their family responsibilities in a vain struggle to fit some unrealistic masculine image. Such men must learn that true masculinity begins with a commitment to Jesus Christ and a sincere desire to follow him guided by his Holy Spirit; that true masculinity acknowledges, accepts, and even encourages the expression of individual differences in both male and female abilities or interests; that a really masculine man views sex as something to be accepted and enjoyed but also controlled. In addition, true masculinity respects women as human beings who are to be treated with loving respect, encouraged in their personal development, guided in their child-rearing activities, and accepted as equal partners in the maintenance of the home. When males start being men again—truly masculine men—marriages and families are almost certain to improve.

NOTES

1. Earnest Larsen, *For Men Only* (Liguori, Mo.: Liguori Publications, 1973), p. 7.

2. Michael Lewis, "Culture and Gender Roles: There's No Unisex in the Nursery," *Psychology Today* 5 (May 1972): 54–57.

3. E. M. Pattison, "Notes on the Current Quest for Gender Identity," *Journal of Religion and Health* 14, no. 2 (1975): 82–95.

4. Wallace Denton, *What's Happening to Our Families?* (Philadelphia: Westminster, 1963), p. 55.

5. S. M. Jourard, "Some Lethal Aspects of the Male Role," in *The Transparent Personality*, rev. ed. (New York: Van Nostrand Reinhold, 1971), pp. 34–41.

6. J. O. Balswick and C. W. Peek, "The Inexpressive Male: A Tragedy of American Society," *The Family Coordinator* (October 1971): 363–68.

7. A. Steinmann and A. J. Fox, *The Male Dilemma: How to Survive the Sexual Revolution* (New York: Aronson, 1974).

8. Denton, *What's Happening to Our Families?* pp. 59–65.

9. Ibid., p. 65.

10. G. F. Gilder, *Sexual Suicide* (New York: Quadrangle, 1973).

11. See Vance Packard, *The Sexual Wilderness* (New York: David McKay, 1968).

12. Pattison, "Notes on the Current Quest for Gender Identity."

13. Previously these guidelines have been presented by the author in somewhat different form in a chapter entitled "Beyond the Marlboro Man," *Lifestyle* (Elgin, Ill.: David C. Cook, 1975).

14. These concepts are presented by Terry Morrison in *Brigade Leader*, Winter 1974, p. 19.

5

A Christian Model
for Sexual Understanding
and Behavior

Harry N. Hollis, Jr.

Several years ago I attended a religious retreat at a state park. A business convention was also being held there, and it had attracted many swingers. At breakfast the next morning, an obviously sleepy male entered the restaurant and approached a woman at the table next to me. "Were you the one?" he queried with a mixture of curiosity and quiet desperation.

"No, it wasn't me," she giggled.

"What's your room number?" he asked.

"112," she answered.

"Well," he asked, "who was the girl in room 118?" And with that he turned and continued to walk through the restaurant, searching desperately for his anonymous sexual partner of the previous night.

To people caught up in such a futile search for meaning, the Christian message brings the good news of freedom under the lordship of Jesus Christ. What these people need

Harry N. Hollis, Jr., is director of Family and Special Moral Concerns, Christian Life Commission of the Southern Baptist Convention. He has the Ph.D. degree from Southern Baptist Theological Seminary and is the author of several books including *Thank God for Sex!* He and his wife Mary Fern have two children.

is to hear the Christian good news about sex. They, and we, need to be able to say, "Thank God for sex."

When did you last hear a prayer thanking God for sex? When did you last offer a prayer thanking God for sex? Most people feel uneasy linking prayer and sex. In spite of the clear teachings of the Bible, they think that sex and holiness are antithetical, that sex and religion do not mix.

As Christians our task is to communicate the biblical good news about sex to a jaded, fearful society. It is not that we have tried a Christian approach which has failed; our society has not really tried a Christian sex ethic at all.

A CHRISTIAN MODEL

The task at hand is to develop a model for sexual understanding and behavior. What I propose is *a* model, not *the* model, and I offer it in the hope that it can lead people to think seriously and act responsibly.

God has acted and is acting in the world as Creator, Judge, and Redeemer, and he calls us to respond with celebration, self-discipline, and love.[1] (There is unity in what God does, and his activity is separated here strictly for the sake of analysis and understanding.)

I will use the word *sex* in a very general sense to refer to everything about a person that has to do with being a male or a female. Sex is not simply the joining of genitals but a basic life force which is involved in all interpersonal relationships. When referring to strictly physical expressions of sex, I will use such terms as *intercourse, petting,* and so on.

SEX AND CELEBRATION

The Bible documents God's activity in the world as Creator (Gen. 1:1; John 1:1–3; Col. 1:15–16). Out of nothing (*creatio ex nihilo*) God created everything. Our bodies are a good part of God's creation; therefore, sex, which is wrapped up with the total human personality, is good. Don't blame sex on the devil; God is responsible for sex. It is good because it is a gift of God. The only "not good" uttered by God during creation concerned the fact that man was alone (Gen. 2:18), and God remedied this by making a female.

Another implication of God's creative activity is that we have unity of personhood. Because we are psychophysical persons, sex is a part of our total personality. We do not have sex; we are sexual beings. To talk about sex only in physical terms is to miss what the Bible teaches. The body and soul are knit together in such a way that one is affected by the other. This unity of personhood stands against casual intercourse because the attempt to limit intercourse to physical involvement and pleasure is contrary to the biblical teachings about the nature of human beings.

God is responsible for the fact that humans are male or female. He planned the sexes (Gen. 1:27; 2:21–22), a reality that points to the relational aspects of sex and identifies as contrary to the biblical witness the idea that sexual equality requires sexual sameness. Some people today seem to prefer unisex to the distinctiveness of maleness and femaleness. This sort of thinking negates God's intention as Creator.

What does God's creation of sex have to do with marriage? Woman was created to be a helper fit for man (Gen. 2:18). The man leaves his parents and enters a "one flesh" union with his wife (Gen. 2:24). The marriage of man and woman is God's intention for creation and is a social structure by which human life in community is maintained, a sacred task to guide us in our work in the world.[2] In the covenant of marriage, the genuine fulfillment of a shared sexual relationship is possible. Sexual expression needs to be experienced in marriage for two people to share with each other their total life experience. Marriage needs sexual expression to provide unity and quality in the covenant.

This does not mean that all people should marry. God's creative intention gives dignity to marriage, but his redemptive actions place limits on marriage. Jesus said that there were some, including himself, who would not marry for the sake of the kingdom (Matt. 19:12). Being unmarried does not make one an asexual being. People called to celibacy and those who simply do not have the opportunity to marry can be fully human by living for others, as Jesus did. Thus Jesus is the model of morality for the unmarried. He lived for others, and he maintained sexual integrity. He did not sin sexually or in any other way.

Marriage is the norm, in spite of these exceptions, and the Creator intends for intercourse to be expressed in the covenant of marriage. There is no justification for intercourse outside of marriage. At least four purposes of intercourse can be found in the Bible: (1) union in one flesh (Gen. 2:24); (2) procreation (Gen. 1:28); (3) pleasure (Prov. 5:18–19); and (4) communication (Gen. 4:1).

What should be our response to these implications of God's creative activity in relation to sex? We can celebrate sex by praising God, accepting self, and respecting other sexual beings.

Praise to the Creator requires the joyful celebration of sex. In Christian communication about sex, we need to link sex with play, laughter, and joyfulness. Celebrating sex means expressing positive attitudes toward sex. When things go wrong with sex, the problem is not with sex, for it is God's good gift. Problems with sex come from people and the manner in which they express sex.

Praise to the Creator also means accepting God's purpose for marriage and intercourse. We can rejoice in the "one flesh" union. We can accept the procreative purpose of intercourse, which means that a physically and emotionally healthy couple should remain childless only for such exceptional reasons as the likelihood of a serious hereditary disease, the dangerous overpopulation of a country, or a period of nuclear war. We must reject the increasingly popular idea that having a child is an inconvenience which married couples should avoid in order to spend their time in more fulfilling ways.

Praise to the Creator can involve the guiltless appreciation and intense enjoyment of the pleasure of intercourse. It can also lead to the privilege of communicating with one's mate through sexual intercourse and sharing the mystery of sex.

Celebrating sex requires a shift of emphasis within the church. The church must proclaim good news about sex. Praising the Creator for sex can also keep us from taking sex too lightly or too seriously. When we see that God has made us sexual beings, we will neither belittle sex nor make it a god.

Response to the Creator involves accepting ourselves as sexual beings and enjoying our humanity and our maleness or femaleness. We dare not be strait-jacketed by society's stereotypes about males and females, but neither do we dare seek to obliterate our male or female distinctiveness. Differences between the sexes are not merely the result of culture; some differences may be innate.

Environment (parents, school, church, society) guides us in sexual self-acceptance, but, as human beings, we have freedom to choose. We are not determined by culture, and we are free to be the male or female sexual beings that God intended.

Responding to the Creator requires respect for others as sexual beings. We can show appreciation for creation by treating others as persons and not things. In marriage this means mutual respect and sensitivity to the sexual needs of one's mate. Manipulation in marriage is a form of prostitution just as devastating as that of the streetwalkers. Premarital behavior must also be based on a mutual respect which stands clearly against the selfish attempts to divorce the pleasure of intercourse from the involvement with an individual as a total personality.

Let us reject that subhuman, unchristian philosophy which says that intercourse outside marriage may be the loving thing to do in some situations. People who say this, be they ministers or whoever, do not know the heartbreak and agony that fornication and adultery so often bring. They have been reading too much fantasy and too little Bible.

Respect for others as sexual beings also requires an end to the male arrogance that has so long been an unhealthy part of our culture. The true quest of all liberation movements should be the freeing of everyone to be the human beings God intended.

SEX AND SELF-DISCIPLINE

The Bible clearly reveals that the Creator of everything is also the Judge (Gen. 3). As Judge, God controls what he has made and condemns the misuse of his creation. He is no angry tyrant but a just governor, sustaining what he has made.

If anyone doubts the confusion about sex and judgment, consider the way Eve is always pictured as a sexy seductress in contemporary advertising. The Fall is repeatedly attributed to sexual misbehavior although the Bible makes it very clear that human estrangement from God is based on the attempt to overthrow God's sovereignty. Rebellion against God can be found not only in sexual expression but in all of life. Given the reality of the Fall, however, sex is a ready place for the expression of sin. Sensual pleasure is not to be condemned, but the excessive preoccupation with the bodily senses leads to the idolatry of pleasure.

Reinhold Niebuhr has pointed out that sensuality often is expressed as excessive self-love, the deification of another person, or the flight into subconsciousness.[3] In sexual behavior, self-love often leads to Don Juan or *femme fatale* manipulation of partners for lustful self-fulfillment. The deification of another leads to an idolatry which is doomed to fail because it cannot deliver what the idolater needs. The attempt to use sexual intercourse as an escape from conscious reality is a misunderstanding of God's intention for sex. Intercourse does not free us from participating in life; instead, by releasing us from tension, it frees us for life.

How do we experience God's judgment in relation to sex? There is shame (Gen. 3:7) which is the result of sin's limitation of the personal manifestation of sex.[4] Judgment is also experienced through anxiety which may come from a guilty conscience or from personal and family tragedies related to sexual misbehavior such as the discovery of a clandestine affair. We experience judgment through longing which means that sin has entered the sexual relation so that we can never find ultimate satisfaction through sexual consummation.[5] Judgment can be seen in the antagonism between the sexes which occurs when the capacity for community is distorted by sin.

Some consider marriage an order of judgment and a remedy against sin. To reduce marriage to a remedy against sin is to misunderstand the nature of marriage. This view sees the wedding ring as a mark of slavery instead of a symbol of celebration and sees sin largely in terms of external acts instead of self-centeredness and rebelliousness. Marriage does serve to bring order and stability to society, and therefore it is a part of judgment in the sense that it protects the goodness of the one-flesh relation and the children who are born to such a union.

How can we respond to what God is doing in the world in relation to judgment and sex? We can acknowledge God's judgment in our own lives, repent and exercise self-discipline, and seek to restrain evil in society.

Our capacity for self-deception finds fertile soil for development in the realm of sexual behavior. We are called, therefore, to acknowledge that God's judgment applies not only to others but also to ourselves. Like Adam and Eve, we blame others for our own disobedience (Gen. 3:12–13). Our tendency to self-deception can be overcome by the recognition and acknowledgment that God who created sex also wills that it be controlled and used for his purposes.

Repentance grows out of an acknowledgment of God's judgment. Too often the Christian community has tried to get people to feel remorse for their sexual sins, but what is needed is a genuine *metanoia,* a turning about-face.

Self-discipline flows out of repentance. Even the discipline of self comes not from self but as a gift from God. Discipline requires us to reject the self's attempt to seek pleasure without giving in return. It necessitates resisting momentary sexual temptations in order to maintain the fidelity of the marriage covenant. It rejects playboy and playgirl focus on paper fantasies which block us from relationships with real human persons.

Not only should we restrain evil in our own lives by accepting the gift of self-discipline, but we are also called to restrain evil in our society.[6] There will be strong objections to attempts to restrain sexual behavior, but we cannot remain indifferent to social distortions of sex in our communities. Sexual expressions are private, but they are not entirely private. The powerful nature of sex and the social implications of sexual behavior combine to make the need for some control and restraint imperative. For example, the attempt to legalize prostitution is an absolutely absurd step in the wrong direction. Legalizing sexual exploitation will not bring sexual health to our society; it will just make us sicker.

In seeking to restrain the misuses of sex, moralism will be of little help. Instead, we must deal with the anxiety and emotional impoverishment which have led to sexual misbehavior. Here psychology and theology can, and indeed must, work together. The spiritual transformation of the individual must be accompanied by an understanding of the psychological dynamics of sex.

Restraining the misuses of sex depends not only on the constructive discipline of individuals but also on changing social structures. For example, individual sex education is often negated by advertising's commercial exploitation of sex. Is it not rather foolish and futile to seek to restrain the misuses of sex while allowing, at the same time, advertising's constant sexual stimulation of the young and those who wish they were young? Furthermore, the linking of sex and violence on television is a national disgrace. We must encourage everyone to write the Federal Communications Commission asking for immediate hearings to air complaints about this exploitation of sex and violence.

The social restraint of sexual misbehavior is no easy matter; yet God is active as Judge and summons us to work through the community of Christian believers to find guidance for this restraint. The Christian response must be neither the imperialism of saints correcting sinners, nor the indulgence of sinners refusing to correct sinners, but involvement where sinners lovingly correct sinners as they are corrected by God.[7]

LOVE AND SEX

Several years ago I taught a seminary course on "The Church and Sexuality." After class one day a student complained, "You are teaching too much about redemption and sex. What people need to hear is judgment. There is just too much permissiveness in this world to talk about forgiveness. We've got to condemn all the sexual immorality. Things are too bad to talk about redemption."

This student incarnates the antisexual bias of our day by interpreting redemption as softness and forgiveness as permissiveness. He fails to see that God's judgment points toward redemption.

A theological statement that concentrates on creation can lead us to be too optimistic about the possibility of correct sexual behavior. Focusing on judgment makes us too pessimistic. A treatment of redemption is needed, therefore, to help us have a balanced realism about sex.

The Bible teaches that the God who creates and judges also redeems and that his work as Creator and Redeemer is inseparable (Isa. 44:24). The motive of God's judgment is redemption, an activity that has implications for us as we seek to understand sex.

In the first place, the fact that the Redeemer graciously offers forgiveness to us has far-reaching significance for sexual understanding and behavior. Before dealing with specific acts of sexual sin in our lives, however, we must first deal with the more basic attitude of pride which estranges us from the Creator. It is rather fruitless to concentrate on specific acts of sin to the neglect of the new life made possible through the work of the Redeemer. When we acknowledge that we have rebelled against God and misused the life that he has given us, we can find forgiveness from the one who was in Christ reconciling the world unto himself (2 Cor. 5:19). Then we can participate in a new life which makes possible the responsible stewardship of sex.

When we accept God's forgiveness, we are in a position to deal with specific sexual sins. These sins often create anxiety which can cause us to seek relief in further acts of sexual exploitation. Forgiveness can cleanse us of the guilt and anxiety that lurk within us when we commit sexual transgressions.

How many discussions have you heard on the Holy Spirit and sex lately? Probably not many. Yet the Holy Spirit convicts us of sin and gives us the power of self-control. Certainly this relates to sexual behavior.

The Holy Spirit enables us to resist an isolated sexual temptation by considering the totality of life: family and fidelity, home and community, persons and covenants. By bringing temptation from darkness to light, the Spirit helps us resist sin. When sin does occur, the Holy Spirit convicts. Further, the Spirit is the source of the love which gives quality to the one-flesh union. Indeed, the Spirit gives the fruits so essential to stable sexual adjustment and community: love, joy, peace, patience, kindness, goodness, faithfulness, gentleness, self-control (Gal. 5:22–23).

A third implication of God's redemptive activity is that he provides us an example of love. God's love is most clearly revealed in the life of Christ and affects our sexual relationships. As we realize that we are loved by God, we are given the capacity to love ourselves and others. Here Christian theology and psychology agree; we learn to love and trust as we are accepted by someone. As we realize that we are accepted by God, we can bring quality to all our relationships.

A final implication of God's redemptive activity is that we are provided with a pattern for community. Redemption makes community possible in our sexual relationships. Although we cannot attain perfect community, we can have a new life and direction which enable us to draw ever closer to the goal of fulfillment we seek. The bridal theology of the Bible is significant in understanding sex, for it gives us a pattern for a covenant relation between people. The metaphor of marriage between God and his people demonstrates the possibility and the significance of such a covenant between a man and a woman (Isa. 62:4–5).

What about redemption and marriage? Redemption means

we can marry, not out of necessity (due to the intention of the Creator), nor to prevent sin (due to the control of the Judge), but in response to the Redeemer who calls us to live a life of love (in the realm of redemption). Marriage has a redemptive purpose in that it serves as an analogy of the relation of Christ and his church.

How can we respond to the Redeemer's actions as they relate to sex? We can respond with forgiveness, love, and participation in the church as a community of hope. By accepting the loving forgiveness of the Redeemer, we are enabled to forgive others. Accepting forgiveness enables us to enjoy sexual pleasure and to associate it with wholesome laughter and good humor. Indeed, laughter helps keep sex in its place.

The Redeemer's forgiveness also encourages us to respond with forgiveness toward others. Indeed, Jesus' treatment of sinners gives us a pattern for such forgiveness. He did not single out sexual sins for special condemnation, but he was a physician to those who were sick with sexual problems. Without approving sexual misconduct, Jesus responded with acceptance and forgiveness. This quality of forgiveness is needed by the church in its ministry to men and women who misuse sex.

We can also respond to the Redeemer with love. In relation to sex, a response of love toward God means gratitude to him for making us sexual beings. It means trusting God to give us guidance in the right use of sex. It means being able to offer a prayer of thanksgiving to God for the enrichment of life that comes from sexual relationships. We can also respond with love for others patterned after the self-giving love of Jesus.

We can respond to God's redemptive activity by participating in the church which is a community of hope. Sharing in such a community can protect us from cynicism and despair about the possibility of controlling sexual behavior. Many are so jaded in sexual matters that they feel there is little hope for restoring beauty and meaning to sexual behavior. The church as a community of hope offers the good news that control is possible through the Holy Spirit, and one hopes that it demonstrates in its life the beauty of healthy sexual relationships.

It is important to respond to the Redeemer by sharing in a community of hope because this will spare us from that hyperindividualism which says that sexual behavior concerns the couple and no one else. In the fellowship of community we come to realize that sexual behavior involves families and societies as well as individuals. This will enhance not hamper intimacy. A couple who lives in isolation from the *koinonia* is not able to bring to intercourse the shared life which makes it an act of completeness and fulfillment. Sharing in a community of hope is also an important response for the unmarried who can find in the church an opportunity for the sublimation of sexual desires.

How can the church be a community of hope in the midst of the sexual pluralism of our culture? The church must share God's requirements in a spirit of forgiveness and love. Without adopting the world's standards, the church must openly listen and minister to people with varied sexual lifestyles. The church can influence society as a whole by holding up the ideal of intercourse within a loving marriage covenant. It can help homosexuals find the aid they need to be the sexual beings God intended. It can work to make certain that the laws not only protect society from sexual offenders but also provide programs for the rehabilitation of these offenders. The church can work for responsible programs of sex education. It can reject discrimination against women and work for human liberation through Christ.

The exploitation of the erotic for financial profit must be diminished. Until something is done to reverse mass media sex miseducation, the church's positive witness will have much less impact. The biggest prostitution problem in our country does not come from the bordellos but from the advertising agencies and business suites where sex fantasies are linked to products in order to increase sales. Consumers share some of the responsibility for such prostitution. The church can foster religious values and cultivate sexual integrity as a way to get at this exploitation.

The church can help parents as they teach their children about sex. Here are some essentials that the church can help parents teach:

1. Sex education should provide correct information about the facts of life as the child is ready to receive this instruction.
2. Sex education can help the child develop a healthy attitude toward sex itself.
3. Sex education should be directed toward self-acceptance and understanding of one's role as a male or female.
4. Sex education can provide an understanding of relationships with other persons.
5. Sex education can assist the child in developing his own value system.[8]

God gave us sex for the enrichment of life, but a funny thing happened to sex on the way to the twentieth century. To be truthful, what happened was not funny at all. Sex got perverted into something dirty and unclean. Therefore, the church needs to scrape off the barnacles of unbiblical tradition and unscientific superstition so that a wholesome Christian view of sex can appear. We cannot afford any longer the excess baggage of negativism. The harm that this heresy has done is immeasurable because it has robbed men and women of the ability to appreciate and enjoy sex as God intended.

At times the church has not been a community of hope in relation to sex. It has sometimes responded to sexual problems with legalism or silence. To offer good news to people, the church must, therefore, relate sex to what God is doing in the world as Creator, Judge, and Redeemer.

I have outlined a model for sexual understanding and behavior. God has acted as Creator, and we are summoned to respond with celebration, self-acceptance, and respect for others. God's actions as Judge require a response of acknowledgment of his judgment, repentance and self-discipline, and the restraint of evil. God has acted as Redeemer, and we are called to respond with forgiveness, love, and participation in the church as a community of hope.

The Bible teaches that Christians have good news about sex to share with society. Through Christ we can celebrate sex, find the power to be sexually responsible, and link love and sexual fulfillment! As we face the future, let us share this good news.

I have a vision of the future, O God,
  When people will express sex as you intend.
I see a time
  When men will stop stripping women of their humanity,
  When women will quit using their bodies to trap men into
    marriage,
  When admen will stop pimping sex to sell products,
  When novels won't be four-hundred-page dirty jokes,
  When children won't have to learn about sex from
    uninformed peers,
  When sex will settle down to its rightful place in life.

But, Lord, I have some questions about sex in the future.

What kind of sexual future is there
  For the prostitute who is old at nineteen?
What hope is there
  For the couple who cannot agree about anything
    including sex?

How can the jaded playboy
  Ever enjoy wholesome and happy play again?
How can there be any gaiety
  For the guilt-ridden gay?
What does the future hold for sex?
  Wild swinging or covenant keeping?
  Licentiousness or wholesomeness?
  Lust or love?
  Prurience or purity?
  Snickers or laughter?
  Bed-hopping or the marriage bed undefiled?

I know, O Lord, that the answers to my questions
Will be determined by the place people give you in the future.

I confess that I fear the problems of the future brave
  new world,
But I celebrate the possibilities of healthier sex tomorrow.

Lord, I know that sex gone wrong will
  Shatter homes,
  Destroy careers,
  Spoil spirits,
  Embitter hearts,
  Cheapen bodies,
  Decay souls.

But I also believe that sex rightly lived will
  Ennoble lives,
  Lift hearts to joy,
  Bring laughter,
  Give birth to ecstasy,
  Lead to enduring love.

What is the future of sex in my life, Lord?
Will it go right or wrong?
It depends on my relationship to you.
Keep sex good in my life.
Make the future a time when I will say:
  "Thank God for sex!"[9]

NOTES

1. H. Richard Niebuhr developed this model in his writings, but he never published an extensive treatment of it in relation to sexual behavior. E. Clinton Gardner and Waldo Beach have applied Niebuhr's model as it relates to ethics. See Gardner, *Biblical Faith and Social Ethics* (New York: Harper & Bros., 1960), pp. 207–47; and Beach, *The Christian Life* (Richmond, Va.: CLC Press, 1966), pp. 38–101.

2. Emil Brunner, *The Divine Imperative,* trans. Olive Wyon (Philadelphia: Westminster Press, 1947), p. 336.

3. Reinhold Niebuhr, *The Nature and Destiny of Man* (New York: Charles Scribner's Sons, 1941) 1:239–40.

4. Emil Brunner, *Man in Revolt,* trans. Olive Wyon (Philadelphia: Westminster Press, 1947), pp. 350–51.

5. Ibid.

6. Beach, *Christian Life,* p. 87.

7. Ibid.

8. For a discussion of these principles, see Harry N. Hollis, Jr., *Getting Rid of the Birds and the Bees* (Nashville: Broadman Press, 1970).

9. Harry N. Hollis, Jr., *Thank God for Sex!* (Nashville: Broadman Press, 1975), pp. 153 ff.

6

Christian Sex Counseling

Ed Wheat

Do you realize the priority God places on sexual union in marriage? This highest priority is seen in God's command to our first ancestors. God told man not to learn evil by experience, and God's second command was on how to relate in marriage. In less than ten seconds God gave a most comprehensive session on marriage and sex counseling which included a summary of all that I will be able to share with you in this chapter.

Genesis 2:24 says, "Therefore shall a man leave his father and his mother, and shall cleave unto his wife: and they shall be one flesh." God had divided the woman from man and now commands them again to become joined together as one. In this brief counseling session, even before any sin and its resulting selfishness had entered the human race, we find three basic commands: (1) When we marry, we are to stop depending on our parents or in-laws so that we will become dependent on each other to satisfy our needs; (2) the

---

Ed Wheat, M.D., is a family physician and practices in Springdale, Arkansas. He is an active Christian layman, teaching three adult Bible classes a week, and lectures frequently to Christian groups on sex and marriage. Dr. Wheat is married and has three daughters.

man is responsible for holding the marriage together by cleaving tightly and inseparably to the wife God has brought to him; and (3) the command is to be joined together in sexual union. In implementing this counsel, the man and the woman were both naked and not ashamed. Originally, sexual union was for companionship and pleasure as at this point in the history of man Adam and his wife apparently were not yet able to bear children. In other words, sex is God's idea, and it was designed for pleasure and delight.

The importance of God's first sex counseling session is emphasized and given an even stronger stamp of approval by the fact that Jesus Christ repeated it precisely in his own brief sex counseling to the religious leaders of his day. "But from the beginning of the creation God made them male and female. For this cause shall a man leave his father and mother, and cleave to his wife; And they twain shall be one flesh: so then they are no more twain, but one flesh. What therefore God hath joined together, let not man put asunder" (Mark 10:6–9).

If Jesus was so emphatic to the leaders of his day about the importance of preserving the marriage union, shouldn't we as Christians today give serious thought to how we can be of specific help to those with problems in the important area of the physical relationship in marriage?

These same commands of God are repeated in Ephesians 5:31, and in 1 Corinthians 7:3–5 the husband is commanded to stop defrauding his wife by refusing to give to her the proper degree of physical pleasure and satisfaction in marriage. The only activity which is to interrupt briefly the normal sex relations between a Christian man and his wife is fasting and prayer. Today this means that one or the other of the marriage partners feels a burden to ask God in prayer to accomplish a specific spiritual ministry in the life of another person.

With this scriptural support for the fact that God instructs every Christian to enjoy sex in marriage, I would like to share with you very specific and intimate information. As a Christian family physician, I have found this information useful in helping couples develop a more dynamic, thrilling, exciting, and satisfying physical relationship in marriage.

PREMARITAL COUNSELING

All of us who counsel young people need to know how to give specific sexual information to every young couple before they become newlyweds.

About eight weeks before marriage, it would be well for every couple to have a complete physical examination. A thoughtful, concerned physician can help remove much of a girl's fear of physical pain due to intercourse. If the pelvic examination reveals a thick or tight hymen, she may wish to have the physician stretch this, or she may want to depend on her personal counselor to give explicit instruction to her fiancé so that he will be able to stretch the hymen after their marriage on the wedding night.

The hymen has been given the name of the mythical god of marriage and is a membrane at the back part of the outside opening of the vagina. It may be relatively tough, or it may even be absent from birth; so its absence is not necessarily an indication of loss of virginity. The opening in the hymen of a virgin is about one inch in diameter and has to be about one and one-half inches in diameter for comfortable intercourse.

At the time of their first intercourse 50 percent of brides say they have some pain but not enough to complain about; 20 percent say they have no pain at all; and 30 percent have rather severe pain.

If a couple chooses to have the husband stretch the hymen on the wedding night, it is very important that a water-soluble lubricant, such as K-Y jelly, be generously applied to the penis and around the vaginal outlet. The husband should assume the man-above position so the penis can be more easily directed downward and toward the back of the vaginal opening. The wife should lift her hips upward to do the thrusting as she will be able to better control the amount of pressure she can tolerate. It may take several trials to penetrate the hymen. If unsuccessful after a few trials, the couple should not keep bruising this area until it is so painful they cannot enjoy their time together. They should just gently and slowly caress each other's genital organs until they are sexually satisfied.

With generous amounts of lubricant on his fingers and with fingernails filed short and smooth, the husband can manually dilate the vaginal opening. He must gently insert one finger into the vagina, then two fingers, using a gradual, firm, downward pressure toward the anus until there is a definite pain and until both these fingers can be easily inserted all the way to the base of the fingers. If this is too painful, it is usually better to be patient until the next day before again attempting well-lubricated introduction of the penis. Most of the pain is from entering too quickly, not giving the muscles around the vagina sufficient time to relax.

If he is not successful after several attempts, she should again consult her physician so he can stretch the hymen. The doctor may sometimes need to make small incisions in the hymen at the back and on each side. This is done in the doctor's office, using a small amount of local anaesthetic. These incisions will heal within a week as will any other small tear in the hymen.

The objectives of newlyweds in the first few weeks of sexual encounters are maximum feminine comfort and maximum masculine control. A couple should not expect much harmony in sexual intercourse for at least a few weeks. At the time of first intercourse, the husband probably should not strive to bring his bride to orgasm with the penis in the vagina because she will have some soreness, and there is no reason to make this worse. On the wedding night, if the penis is inserted, the husband should have his orgasm quickly, withdraw the penis, and proceed to gently but persistently stimulate his bride's clitoris lightly with well-lubricated fingers for as long as thirty minutes to give her the opportunity to try to achieve orgasm. He should not stop unless his bride finds this stimulation irritating or annoying.

The couple should be warned that when the hymen is stretched or torn, there often is some bleeding but usually no more than one or two teaspoons. If this bleeding continues, or if there is as much as one tablespoon of blood, they should not be afraid but look carefully for the exact spot that is bleeding and hold a tissue on that spot with firm pressure. There is no bleeding that cannot be stopped in this way. She may leave the tissue in place about twelve hours and then soak it loose in a warm bath to avoid new bleeding. She may resume having intercourse the next day. If there is bleeding again, just repeat the local pressure.

The urethra, a tube which runs just beneath the pubic bone, is the outlet for the urine from the bladder. The urethral opening is about one-half inch above the vaginal opening and entirely separate from it. It resembles a rounded dimple containing a tiny slit. In the first few days after marriage the urethra can be easily bruised unless plenty of lubrication is provided for the penis in the vagina.

Bruising of the urethra produces what is commonly called "newlywed cystitis" or "honeymoon cystitis," which is characterized by pain in the bladder area, blood in the urine, and rather severe burning when the urine passes. This is an indication that injury to the urethra has allowed bacteria to grow. Bacteria may ascend to produce a severe bladder infection called "cystitis." Cystitis clears up and pain is alleviated much quicker with prescription medication and by drinking more fluids. It is often helpful in prevention of cystitis to urinate a few minutes after each intercourse to help get rid of bacteria which may have been introduced into the urethra.

Every couple, regardless of any previous sexual experience, should use a surgical lubricant often during the first few weeks to help prevent this painful condition caused by bruising. To insist on the use of this lubricant may be the most useful sexual advice a counselor can give newlyweds.

SEXUAL SENSITIVITY AND RESPONSE

Called the trigger of female desire, the clitoris is the most keenly sensitive point a woman has for sexual arousal, and as far as we know, this is its only function. There are husbands and wives who do not know the location of this vital organ or do not even know its name—and these are not uneducated people. The word *clitoris* comes from the Latin word meaning "that which is closed in," and its shaft, which is about one-half to one inch long, is closed in by a foreskin at the peak of the labia about two inches in front of the entrance to the vagina and above the urinary opening or urethra. At its outer end is a small, rounded body about the size of a pea, which is called the glans, from a Latin word meaning "acorn."

Persistent, gentle stimulation of the clitoris, either directly or indirectly, will produce an orgasm in nearly all women. For this reason, many thought the physical location of the clitoris on the body, so it would come into contact with the penis, was the only important thing in achieving orgasm. Many operations have been done to further expose the clitoris, but this surgery seldom helps attain orgasm. With our present knowledge, this surgery should never be done until information such as we are sharing here has been learned thoroughly and applied in the sex relationship. There is no difference in actual physical sensation from orgasm by manual clitoral stimulation and that from sexual intercourse.

The clitoris usually enlarges some when caressed, though in many women this enlargement is not detectable since it occurs in diameter, not in length. The size of the clitoris or its degree of enlargement has nothing to do with sexual satisfaction or sexual capacity.

When the clitoris is first stimulated in foreplay, light, gentle, and slow caressing of the very end probably will give the most pleasant sensation. In a few seconds, this area may become overly sensitive and even irritated, and stroking further back on the shaft or gentle movement of the labia minora may be most pleasurable. Some wives may even prefer to be loved and stimulated for a while in some entirely different erotic area such as the breasts, inner thighs, even by stroking the back, the ear lobes, or a combination of areas.

Building sexual tension or excitement after actual introduction of the penis is an ability that a woman can seek and learn. She must put anticipation foremost in her mind, surrender to her own natural drives, and seek emotional and physical stimulation until this tension climaxes in release. Vigorous thrusting as soon as the male organ enters the vagina is almost a guarantee that the wife's sensation will be blurred and that excitement will actually decline.

The art of love is largely a savoring of each phase of the experience, seeking maximum perception of sensation, rather than working and hurrying toward release. Achieving orgasm is the very thing that ends the sexual enjoyment. Every physical union should be a contest to see which partner can outplease the other. Sexual intercourse will always be a joyful affirmation of two people's common life or a revelation of the defects and will either draw people together or push them apart.

The wife views the sex act as a part of the total relationship with her husband. This means that every meaningful, fully enjoyable sex act really begins with a loving, attentive attitude which may begin hours or even days before. This requires both partners to assume the responsibility for giving their total self—physically, emotionally, and spiritually —so that the sex act becomes a dynamic technique to express fully unselfish love one for the other.

Cleanliness is a necessity for greatest sexual enjoyment. Before any sexual union, it is very important for both husband and wife to realize that there is ample soap in the world for bathing and there is a sufficient amount of toothpaste available. There is no shortage of shaving cream or blades for both, and there are nail clippers and nail files for careful smoothing of the husband's fingernails.

The sexual response to effective stimulation for a man and a woman is actually very similar in duration, in intensity, in overall pattern, in bodily or muscular responses, and in physical sensations; but there may be a different intensity or timing for any two specific individuals.

There is no great superiority in simultaneous orgasm. This is an individual matter toward which each couple should aim, but it is not something to strive for. There is a unique joy in giving all the skill you have to pleasing your partner without regard to when either will reach orgasm.

One may find it helpful in counseling to describe the sexual response in terms of the following four divisions: (1) initial excitement, lasting usually less than one minute; (2) gradually increasing tensions, ideally lasting about ten to twenty minutes or longer and encompassing actual insertion of the penis into the vagina; (3) orgasm, sometimes referred to as climax or sexual release; and (4) relaxation.

The very first sign of sexual arousal in men is erection of the penis, and this occurs within a few seconds after being triggered by direct stimulation, a stimulating sight, or an erotic train of thought.

The length of the nonstimulated penis varies greatly, but the erect penis is almost always between five and seven inches long. The size of the penis has nothing to do with how much either partner enjoys intercourse since only the outer two inches of the vagina contain tissue which is stimulated by pressure on the inside. Many men think deep penetration of the penis gives the wife greater stimulation, but it is actually better contact with the clitoris or stretching downward of the labia by the base of the penis that increases, or may increase, her stimulation to the time of her climax.

The most stimulating area to touch on the penis is the area along the underside of the shaft and the part where the head joins the shaft. Four things will increase the physical intensity of a man's orgasm: (1) wait at least twenty-four hours after previous orgasm to allow the body to store a larger volume of seminal fluid; (2) lengthen the foreplay period so that the penis can remain erect at least twenty minutes; (3) strengthen the muscular contractions and increase the force of thrusting during orgasm; and (4) increase the imagination factor by seeing and feeling his wife's estatic response to his knowledgeable, skillful, physical stimulation to the point of her maximum physical pleasure. This is an expansion of 1 Peter 3:7 which speaks of the sexual union when it says each husband should dwell with his wife according to knowledge. In other words, each husband should certainly be the world's greatest authority on what pleases his wife.

For the most intense physical sensation in orgasm for both husband and wife, there should be twenty minutes or more from the beginning of the excitement phase until the time of orgasm. Much of this time may be spent in building sexual tensions by foreplay. Many husbands will need to learn more self-control, but usually the duration of actual penile containment should be from five to fifteen minutes. Be careful, however, not to allow these figures to make one a sexual clock-watcher. Each couple will have their own ideal timing for each sexual encounter, but they can significantly enrich their pleasure by considerably lengthening the time of foreplay.

The very first sign of sexual arousal in the female is the moistening of the vagina with a slippery, thin, transparent lubricating fluid. This usually occurs after ten to thirty seconds of stimulation. Unfortunately, many men think copious lubrication is the signal the wife is ready for insertion of the penis. Actually she is just beginning to be excited.

The time of excitement for the woman is begun by foreplay, but the term *foreplay* is misleading if one considers it a warm-up before the real game. In most instances foreplay is almost all of the real game. Unfortunately, many couples are not aware of their great need for foreplay. In foreplay, there is really no system to know, only another person to know. Never let foreplay be mechanical.

In sexual stimulation, one woman's arousal may be another's boredom. This is what makes the love relationship in marriage so private a matter between those who can express their affection in ways which are meaningful to the other.

The vast majority of women are stimulated, not merely by receiving affection, but also by giving it. Each woman should take full part in foreplay by stimulating her husband before sexual union, beginning by very gently stroking the underside of the penis, the inner thighs, the area between the scrotum and anus, the scrotum itself, or wherever her husband directs.

During the time of the woman's increasing sexual tension, there is engorgement and swelling of the labia minora and the outer one-third of the vagina. As a result, the vaginal diameter may be reduced as much as 50 percent. This is usually the most easily observed physical sign that the woman is ready for insertion of the penis.

Every woman may follow a little different pattern, but

the most important single determination for beginning the actual sexual union is when the wife says to begin. Many sexual frustrations could be solved if husbands and wives talked a little bit more.

Sometimes even after the entrance of the penis, the man may need to continue to caress the clitoris with his fingers. The period from the time of increasing stimulation to orgasm is a period usually needing persistent, progressive, and continuing intensification of clitoral stimulation.

The major observable feature of the female orgasm is a series of rhythmic contractions of the muscles of the outer one-third of the vagina called the Pubococcygeus or PC muscle group. The first few contractions occur at intervals about one second apart; then intervals become longer, and the intensity tapers off. A mild orgasm usually gives three to five of these contractions, and an intense orgasm may give eight to twelve.

The wife does not necessarily begin to relax immediately after the initial orgasm. If she desires, with continuing stimulation, she may be able to reach promptly a second orgasm or even a series of up to ten or twelve orgasms before entering the relaxation period. Almost all women desire continuing direct stimulation of the clitoris all the way through each orgasmic experience and will usually stop orgasm if stimulation is discontinued.

In counseling conferences on sexual adjustment, some couples ask, "What do you do when intercourse is finished?" During the remainder of the relaxation phase, it is desirable for the husband to continue tenderly to show love to his wife by hugs, kisses, and gentle love pats. He should continue to make her aware of his appreciation for her as they lie close in each other's arms and just enjoy each other's presence. This makes for a much smoother transition to complete relaxation together.

At this point, I would like to mention the need for privacy.

Each couple, in considering buying or building a home, should try to arrange to have a master bedroom with connecting bath isolated as much as possible and soundproofed from other occupied rooms. Every master bedroom must have a good lock, controlled from the inside, for many couples need assured security from any invasion to allow their full concentration for maximum sexual enjoyment. Also, no couple, under any circumstances, should allow any age child to sleep in the room with them, except perhaps a new baby for the first six months or less. Every small child should be trained never to disturb mother and daddy, night or day, when their bedroom door is locked. Speaking of privacy, sex pleasures or problems should never be discussed with friends or family, and no one should joke about any of these private matters.

SEX AND THE OLDER MARRIED COUPLE

There is a great emphasis in our entire society today on young people to the extent that it seems that most literature on sex would imply that sex is only for the young. Christian leaders should be aware that most of the stability of our churches rests on older men and women, and we should try to keep a strong love relationship in our older couples.

Many aging women have the false notion that they will lose interest and pleasure in sex as they go on past the menopause. This simply is not true. There are some changes in the sexual response, but this certainly does not mean sex is not enjoyed as much as ever. Many women experience increasing physical pleasure because of their greater freedom from family responsibility and because of their relief over concern for pregnancy.

After menopause, intercourse may be painful for some women because the lower hormone levels cause the vaginal walls to become thin and less elastic, and thus more easily irritated by sexual intercourse. This is called senile vaginitis and can be avoided by taking sufficient estrogen or by using a vaginal cream locally which contains estrogen which is absorbed there by the surface of the vagina. Also, there may be a need for more artificial lubricant. I have noted that women who have satisfying sexual intercourse once or twice a week all through the menopausal years have fewer symptoms of hot flashes, irritability, and nervousness and even much less change in the vaginal walls, even with little or no hormone replacement.

Few older couples come for sex counseling, so it becomes even more important to establish good sex relations in our younger couples. Each couple who is frequently enjoying good sexual functioning should go into the mature years expecting to continue physical enjoyment with each other with the understanding that some of the timing and frequency of response will change, but this does not mean the sexual fun is over. With close attention to details in how to stimulate each other, the older couple may even be able to reawaken sexual responses they thought were lost long ago.

There is a change in the aging husband's pattern of response in intercourse. Body processes slow down with age, but they do not stop. There is no reason why many men cannot continue an active sex life into their eighties or nineties. Probably the greatest obstacle each has to overcome is the fear of losing his ability to get or keep an erection; then he must avoid more fears when sometimes he does fail. It usually takes longer to get an erection. This definitely does not mean that sexual activity is going to stop—only that there is a change.

There may now need to be a more attentive concern by the wife to stimulate the penis to keep her older husband aware of her sexual interest and love and concern for his satisfaction. She may need to learn the skill of inserting the penis when it is not fully erect, knowing the first few thrusts will often add much stimulation to get more of an erection. Because of the lessened demand for ejaculation, many older husbands find they have really become much better lovers and are able to allow their wives to feel sexually in ways they were never allowed before.

The most important single aspect in prolonging a man's sexual ability into old age is for him to realize that he does not need to ejaculate every time there is intercourse. Up to this time, both partners always felt ineffective if the husband did not ejaculate, but as age advances, the husband should never force an ejaculation when he does not feel a need for it. If he does this, his powers to get and keep an erection will diminish.

With even the most skillful prolonged vaginal stimulation by the penis in the vagina by a husband with excellent ejaculatory control, there is basically no difference in the physical intensity of the orgasm itself for the husband or wife from that of clitoral stimulation alone or even by self-stimulation.

TOTAL ONENESS

There is really a far greater dimension to the sexual relationship for the mature Christian couple who have a total commitment to Jesus Christ and flowing from that a realization of their own security in spiritual and physical oneness, with a total commitment and excitement found only in each other, knowing this is for as long as they live and even forever. This genuine total oneness and completeness somehow cannot really be explained; it must be experienced. The prolonged, controlled, properly and lovingly executed, mutually satisfying sexual union is God's way of demonstrating to us a great spiritual truth of the greatest love story ever told, of how Jesus Christ is intimately related to and loves the church. We see this clearly in Ephesians 5:31–32:

"For this cause shall a man leave his father and mother, and shall be joined unto his wife, and they two shall be one flesh. This is a great mystery, but I speak concerning Christ and the church."

When this type of relationship exists, the sexual union becomes even an act of worship. As the sex act is finished, many times both husband and wife will want to praise the Lord and have communion with him in prayer, thanking him for each other and for the complete intimate love that they have shared.

This type of relationship can only begin in one way. Each person individually must recognize that Jesus Christ as God chose to come to this planet earth to be born the son of a virgin, to live a perfect life without a single act of sin. By his own choice, he went to the cross to shed his blood, to die as a substitute in our place, bearing our sins and taking the punishment for those sins which was death.

As proof for all the world for all time to see that he is God, in three days he arose from the dead and bodily walked among his disciples and about five hundred other eye-witnesses at one time as declared in 1 Corinthians 15:1–7. Later in the resurrection body as the God-man, he ascended into heaven and has promised in John 14:2–3 that he is preparing a place for us and will come again to receive us unto himself.

Believing these facts about our Lord Jesus Christ, each person must personally place all his trust, hope, and confidence in Jesus Christ as his Savior and sin-bearer. By taking this simple step of faith, a person becomes a child of God and receives a new nature which is capable of giving him the type of love relationship that can solve any marriage problem and bring the physical, emotional, and spiritual oneness God designed for the Christian marriage.

I have seen God work out every conceivable problem in his children, and I have become absolutely convinced that he can work out any sexual problem a couple may have. The couple must first admit they have a problem, and no matter what it is, each must admit that much of it is his own fault. There may have built up in them some personal guilt, resentment, bitterness, or jealousy either toward each other or toward their parents or their background. This may involve recognizing the principle found in Hebrews 12:14–15, "Follow peace with all men, and holiness, without which no man shall see the Lord: Looking diligently lest any man fail of the grace of God; lest any root of bitterness springing up trouble you, and thereby many be defiled." A couple should be urged not to let any bitterness, resentment, past failures, or past hurts disturb the most important relationship they can have in life, that is, the relationship with one's own husband or wife.

Once both recognize their own individual responsibility in the sexual problem, they should confess to God any sin of resentment, false modesty, apathy, indifference, fear, hatred, ignorance or pride, using 1 John 1:9: "If we confess our sins, he is faithful and just to forgive us our sins, and to cleanse us from all unrighteousness." They should then make a deliberate effort to forsake that sin and look to the Lord to provide true information which will guide them to a solution.

In this chapter I have briefly given material to be used in instructing a Christian couple in ways to enhance their enjoyment in the sex relationship. Advice has also been offered to newlyweds and to aging couples to help avoid sexual maladjustments.

If further specific information is needed to deal with sexual problems which have already developed, I have made a two-cassette album providing three hours of specific instruction entitled *Sex Technique and Sex Problems in Marriage*. These cassettes have been found useful to give or loan to Christian couples. As the couple listens to these cassettes together, there is specific instruction for their own solution to the most common sexual problems: frigidity, lack of sexual desire, painful intercourse, vaginismus, pelvic congestion, premature ejaculation, and impotence.

Many pastors are now loaning a set of these cassettes to each couple to whom they give premarital counseling. They usually encourage the couple to wait until about two weeks before the wedding to listen and ask that the cassettes be taken with them on their honeymoon to hear again.

I encourage counselors to continue to provide information and help in the troubled marriages of those Christian couples God sends to you. If parents do not have a working, practical knowledge of that which is good and exciting in their own sexual relationship, they will not be able to share information with their sons and daughters before their marriage that will help them achieve and maintain the very best relationship in marriage. Those who function in the role of a Christian counselor should consider this not as sex education, but as love education, and this always ideally begins in the Christian's own home.

SUGGESTED RESOURCES

Drakeford, John W. *Made for Each Other.* Sexuality in Christian Living Series. Nashville, Tenn.: Broadman Press, 1973.

Florio, Anthony. *Two to Get Ready.* Old Tappan, NJ: Fleming H. Revell, 1974.

LaHaye, Tim. *How to Be Happy Though Married.* Grand Rapids, Mich.: Zondervan, 1968.

———. *The Act of Marriage.* Grand Rapids, Mich.: Zondervan, 1975.

Miles, Herbert J. *Sexual Happiness in Marriage.* Grand Rapids, Mich.: Zondervan, 1967.

Miles, Herbert J. *Sexual Understanding before Marriage.* Grand Rapids, Mich.: Zondervan, 1971.

Petersen, J. Allan. *Before You Marry.* Wheaton, Ill.: Tyndale House.

———. *Two Become One.* Wheaton, Ill.: Tyndale House.

Rice, Shirley. *Physical Unity in Marriage.* Norfolk, Va.: Norfolk Christian Schools, 1973.

Small, Dwight. *Christian, Celebrate Your Sexuality.* Old Tappan, NJ: Fleming H. Revell, 1974.

———. *Design for Christian Marriage.* Old Tappan, NJ: Fleming H. Revell, 1959.

Taylor, Jack. *One Home under God.* Nashville, Tenn.: Broadman Press.

Timmons, Tim. *1 + 1.* Christian Family Life, 64 Coachlight Drive, Little Rock, Ark.

Wheat, Ed. *Sex Techniques and Sex Problems in Marriage.* This cassette may be ordered by addressing Ed Wheat, M.D., Springdale, Ark. 72764

Wright, H. Norman. *Communication: Key to Your Marriage.* Glendale, Cal.: Regal-Gospel Light, 1974.

7

A Biblical View
of Homosexuality
Dennis F. Kinlaw

In any serious philosophical discussion, what is unsaid is
often more important than what is affirmed. When one
speaks of what the Scriptures teach, this is even more true,
for the assumptions one brings to the discussion are determinative. Over the last century biblical criticism has so
fragmented the consensus in the church on the Scripture
that extreme candor is needed for meaningful dialogue.
Therefore, it is appropriate for me to spell out my pre-
suppositions.

My conviction is that the Scriptures give us, not just the
thinking of ancient Hebrew prophets and Christian apostles,
but the actual Word of God. In the Bible we can find the
attitude and mind of God on issues of ultimate concern for
man. Given over different periods of human history from
numerous writers, the Scriptures reveal a basic integrity and
unity that come from a common origin. The message tran-

Dennis F. Kinlaw is president of Asbury College in Wilmore, Kentucky. He earned the M.A. and Ph.D. degrees from Brandeis University. Before entering the academic profession, Dr. Kinlaw pastored
churches in North Carolina and New York. He and his wife Elsie have
five children.

scends the social, cultural, and religious limitations of the spokesmen and authentically and correctly communicates the divine mind as God has seen fit to disclose it to man.

This means that the Scriptures have universal significance and are binding upon all. They communicate to us truth inaccessible elsewhere to human discovery about the meaning and purposes of human life, human relationships, and human institutions. The Scriptures are thus normative, but more. They provide a key that enlightens and liberates. That key, not found in the creation, is lovingly disclosed in Scripture by a beneficent Father. What society, the state, and the church have to say about homosexuality are of interest. Only what God says is really binding. That is to be found in Scripture.

A second supposition is basic to this chapter: Homosexuality can be dealt with adequately only in relation to the broader teaching of Scripture on sexuality. Before we understand the problem of homosexuality, we must know the teaching of Scripture on sexuality generally and how homosexuality relates to the nature and purposes of masculinity and femininity. Our attention cannot be confined simply to the limited passages that deal directly with our subject.

The seedbed for all Scripture is laid in the story of the creation and the Fall. The importance of our subject is seen in that two passages in the account of creation deal with human sexuality. These (Gen. 1:26–27, 2:18–25) are determinative. A careful study of these and of the rest of the Scripture reveals their seminal character. The pattern is established and adjudged good (1:31). From then until the close of the biblical corpus it is the assumed norm.

It is obvious even from a superficial reading of these chapters that the character of Adam's and Eve's sexuality was not a result of chance. No biological or social accident, Adam's masculinity and Eve's femininity are recorded as resulting from a deliberate divine plan. The sexual variation in Eve was planned specifically to meet basic needs predesigned in Adam (Gen. 2:18 ff.). It resulted from a *special* and premeditated divine act (Gen. 2:21–23). Eve's femininity had to do with her God-ordained role and was an essential part of her personhood as God created her. This paralleled the fact that Adam was created with a defined masculinity and that his limitation was an essential part of his personhood. Male and female God created them (Gen. 1:27), and their sexual differentiation was necessary for the unity designed in what Scripture calls "one flesh." The basic social unit, not the individual but the married couple, demanded sexual definition and variation. Part of the mystery here is that the Scriptures seem to indicate that this sexual variation may even have its basis in the differentiation within the triune godhead. "Let us make man in our image, after our likeness; . . . So God created man in his own image, in the image of God created he him; male and female he created them" (Gen. 1:26–27, RSV). Without question, man in the dual unity of the "one flesh" of monogamous marriage is made in the image of God. Little wonder that the Scripture calls this "good" (Gen. 1:31) and henceforth considers it normative. No hint of sexual instability or variation, inversion or bisexuality is found. The pattern is laid and attributed to God.

Some may feel this places undue significance on an old Hebrew story. Jesus apparently would not have felt this way. When asked about divorce, he turned to this passage for the norm. He reminded them that "at the beginning" God made them male and female, that conjugal union was really something God had established, that it had a claim on a man's loyalty second only to his responsibility to God, and that the dissolution of that union except on grounds of physical infidelity is sin (Matt. 19:1–12; Mark 10:1–12). The pattern for Christ is that presented in Genesis.

The Apostle Paul likewise finds the pattern there. In 1

Corinthians 6:12–20 and Ephesians 5:21–33, he appeals to Genesis 2:18–25 for a divinely established norm. The union of one male and one female in a mysterious and binding oneness is based on their sexual particularities.

It is obvious that Jesus and Paul both felt they were dealing with a matter of gravest significance. The Old Testament pronounces the strongest penalties for sexual irregularities. One's membership in the covenant community and even physical life itself could be forfeited for transgression here. Jesus extends the complications produced by sexual sin into the next life. Lust is enough to bring one to eternal perdition (Matt. 5:27–32). Paul assures his readers that those who misuse their sexuality will be deprived of any place in the kingdom of God (1 Cor. 6:9–10). Old Testament temporal sanctions against forbidden sexual activity now are made eternally significant and damning. And in the final two chapters of Revelation (21:8 and 22:15) the sexually immoral are outside the eternal city suffering the pains of the lost. What one does with one's sexuality is seen as a concern of God. This good gift is a stewardship from him for which he holds one responsible and for which he has laid down a prescribed pattern. To violate his will is to tamper with his purposes and to necessitate his judgment.

The basic character of this pattern and the unitary commitment of Scripture to it is dramatically seen in the use of the marriage relationship as an analogy of the relation between Israel and Yahweh and the church and Christ. The consistency with which adultery and idolatry are associated suggests that these two things are irrevocably related in the mind of God. A quick glance at the Hebrew lexicon reveals that the Hebrew *zanah*, "to commit fornication or to play the harlot," is used in Exodus, Leviticus, Numbers, Deuteronomy, Judges, Kings, Chronicles, Psalms, Isaiah, Jeremiah, Ezekiel, and Hosea to describe idolatrous activities. The intimate relationship between immorality and idolatry is almost omnipresent within the Scripture.

Always, though, the framework is one in which one nation, Israel, is described as in covenant with one God, Yahweh. Israel is always the bride and plays the role of Eve while Yahweh is the husband and plays the role of Adam. In the New Testament the picture is the same in that the church is the bride of Christ. From Jesus' description of his generation as "adulterous" (Matt. 12:39, 16:4) to the picture of the great harlot in Revelation 17:1 ff., the analogy of sexual immorality is used to picture the evil of idolatry. It is not the unfaithfulness of friend to friend or even lover to lover but wife to husband.

But what of homosexuality? Is it necessarily evil? Cannot a loving homosexual relationship be good? There is not a line of Scripture to support the idea that homosexuality is not a radical departure from the divine plan. Actually there are not a great many explicit references to homosexual practices in the Scriptures. The biblical writers apparently felt no great necessity to speak in detail about such. The establishment of the God-designed norm for God-created people was enough to make the anomalous character of homosexuality obvious.

Two passages from Paul are quite explicit. 1 Corinthians 6:9 tells us that the *malakoi* and the *arsenokoitai* along with the fornicators, adulterers, thieves, greedy, drunkards, slanderers, and swindlers will have no place in the kingdom of God. Arndt and Gingrich define *malakoi* as soft, effeminate persons, especially "catamites, men and boys who allow themselves to be misused homosexually" and *arsenokoitai* as "male homosexuals, pederasts, sodomites."[1]

In his first letter to Timothy, Paul tells us that the law is not made for good men but for evil men and lists the *arsenokoitai* along with adulterers, slave traders, liars, perjurers, ordinary murderers, patricides, and matricides (1 Tim. 1:8–11). It would be difficult for Paul to make his position clearer. Sexual relations between two people of the same sex are unacceptable to God and provoke his wrath.

Perhaps the passage most commonly cited from the New Testament is Romans 1:26–27. Here we are told that rejection of the true God led ultimately to the basest manifestations of human passion. Again idolatry and sexual immorality are related. Idolatrous women exchanged natural relations for unnatural ones (v. 26). Men abandoned natural relations with women for "indecent acts with other men." To lose the right relationship between the creature and the Creator led to wrong relationships between the sexes. Stability in nature is evidently seen and based upon stability in Christ.

Many attempts have been made to reinterpret this passage and find something other than the seemingly obvious references to homosexuality. Some see Paul's reference to women exchanging natural relationships for unnatural ones as nothing more than variations in coital position or method.[2] This hardly seems to merit refutation. Troy Perry argues that the key words are *changing* and *leaving* and that this passage cannot refer to homosexuals since to change or to leave heterosexuality one must be a heterosexual.[3] Again, this seems to be refusing to face the obvious.

Though D. S. Bailey attempts to be sympathetic to the homosexual plight, he acknowledges that Paul is alluding in verse 26 to homosexual acts between females and in verse 27 to the depravities that were common in first-century Rome where homosexual activities played a significant part, as depicted in the *Satyricon* of Petronius and the "epigrams" of Martial.[4]

It must be noted how this passage assumes the divinely established stability of man's sexual orientation in that it was only when men turned their backs upon God that their affinity for the divinely planned way in sexual relationships was forsaken. If men lose God, Paul is saying, men not only do not know who God is, they no longer know their own identity and nature. Homosexuality is thus *perversion* that develops when the knowledge of the Author of the pattern is lost.

Some try to make the thrust of this passage simply a protest against lust, saying that lust is as possible within a heterosexual relationship as within a homosexual one and that this is Paul's concern. What they forget is that sexual relations within the marriage bond are not seen as sinful but good (Song of Sol., 1 Cor. 7:1-5) while sexual relations between two persons of the same sex is evil. The Scripture will have nothing to do with such a suggestion as that of John von Rohr: "So now the explicit statement can be ventured, that the sinfulness of homosexuality is not to be found in the fact that it is *homo*-sexuality but rather in the fact that it is homo-*sexuality* in the midst of man's disordered state, where all sexuality becomes an instrument of his lust as well as of his love."[5] Scripture never condemns sexuality, only those sexual practices which are contrary to the divine plan.

The assumption behind Romans 1 is that there is a natural sexual order that originated with God, that it is good, and that men have forsaken God, rejected his way, and changed the correct order for a false one that is destructive and brings its own dissolution.

Some current writers would try to place these three Scriptures with their condemnation of homosexual activities in the same category with Pauline instructions about women being silent in the church, covering their heads when they pray, and not wearing jewelry (1 Tim. 2:11-12; 1 Cor. 11:5).[6] This simply reflects an inability to differentiate between passing and changing expressions of Christian propriety and abiding moral principles that are rooted in the nature of things. At no point does Paul ever relate these relativities to an unchanging moral order. He is very clear though about the eternal seriousness of violating the *order of creation* such as the order basic to human sexual relations.

References to homosexuality in Leviticus 18:22 and 20:13 cannot be placed in the same category as the dietary laws of Leviticus[7] any more than can the laws of incest, adultery, and murder. There is a difference between eating pork and premeditated murder, even in ancient Israel. The fact that both are forbidden in the same book does not equate them. When Leviticus says that one shall not lie with mankind as with womankind, that it is an abomination (Lev. 18:22, 20:13), it is expressing a moral judgment that never changes in Scripture.

One cannot ignore the possibility that these passages in Leviticus define *abomination* for Revelation 21:27 just as Deuteronomy 23:17–18 may give us the meaning of *dogs* in Revelation 22:15. The equation of *abomination* (Revelation 21:27) with homosexuality and *dogs* with those who engage in homosexual practices cannot be established absolutely from Scripture. The ultimate consequences of homosexual activity are the same throughout Scripture as those who do the *abominable* in Revelation 21:27 and those who live like *dogs* in Revelation 22:15. Of that, there is no question.

A similar word must be spoken about *qedēshīm* and *qedōshōth* of the Old Testament (Deut. 23:17–18; 1 Kings 14:22–24, 15:12, 22:46; 2 Kings 23:7). That they were male and female temple prostitutes cannot be denied. Did a male temple prostitute confine his sexual activities to female patrons? Bailey has suggested such.[8] To me, such argument to protect homosexual activities from biblical condemnation does not seem to merit serious rebuttal. The thrust of the Scriptures is clear. Sexual activity is intended for a male and a female within the bonds of marriage. All sexual intercourse between persons outside this bond, whether between persons of the same sex or of the opposite, is an abomination in the sight of God and evokes his wrath. Anything that ignores this is game playing.

Two other passages of Scripture merit our attention, and these are related. The first is Jude 6–8, and the latter is the Sodom and Gomorrah story in Genesis 19. Jude is addressing the problem of godless men who have slipped in among believers and are turning the grace of God into licensed immorality. He then cites three examples of those turned aside to destruction: Israel in the wilderness, the angels that fell, and Sodom and Gomorrah (vv. 5–7). He condemns Sodom and Gomorrah for turning themselves to sexual immorality and to the pursuit of "strange flesh" (*sarkos* and *heteras*). Traditionally this has been understood as the practice of "unnatural vice."[9] This, of course, fits the tradition that the prime sin of Sodom was homosexuality.

Bailey and others have made great effort to prove there is nothing in the Genesis account to justify the charge of homosexuality against Sodom.[10] He relates Jude's second and third examples, the charge against the Sodomites with the charge against the angels (one wonders if he would also relate these two to the charge against Israel in the wilderness), and insists that "strange flesh" refers not to homosexual activities but to sexual activities between supernatural and human beings. This argument he bases on references in the *Book of Jubilees* and the *Testament of Naphtali*. Apart from the fact that the church has never attributed to these books canonical character or authority, it should be noted that the basic argument against cohabitation between angels and mortals is exactly the argument inherent in Scripture against homosexuality. Men are not made for men, nor women for women, any more than angels were made for mortals or mortals for angels. To use Bailey's own language, both are a "breach of the universal principle of order established by the Creator."[11] What we have in either case is, to use his words again, "the lawless violation of the bounds" appointed by the Lord. In either case, Jude constitutes a valid even if indirect argument against homosexuality.

If, of course, Jude has "revelation" character, it provides a key to the true interpretation of the Sodom story. Certainly there were factors in Sodom's provoking God's wrath other than unnatural sexual activity, but it is impossible to accept Bailey's dogmatic affirmation that the Sodom story has *nothing* to do with homosexuality. His hope that "we shall soon hear the last of Sodom and Gomorrah in connection with homosexual practices" seems unrealistic.[12]

The fact is that Hebrew scholars have normally understood the use of the word *to know* in Genesis 19:5 in a carnal way. The Hebrew lexicon of Brown, Driver, and Briggs cites the use of the verb *to know* in verse 5 as an example of the carnal knowledge of Lot's visitors by their neighbors while the use in verse 8 is seen as meaning carnal knowledge of Lot's daughters by Lot's neighbors.[13] The use of the same word when Lot offers his daughters as that used when the neighbors demand the visitors at least necessitates considering its use in verse 5 as having sexual meaning just as it does in other passages in Genesis (see Gen. 4:1, 17, 25; 24:16; 38:26).

The prime argument against homosexuality lies, as we have seen, not in isolated texts nor in a particular interpretation of the Sodom story, but in the biblical view of the divine purposes of sexuality. The norm was established in Genesis 1 and 2 and is assumed throughout the rest of Scripture. Woman was made for man, and one woman for one man, just as man was made for woman. Human beings were made for God, the one God, Yahweh, and for him alone. The violation of either of these norms puts a person in opposition to the God who created us.

It is not our province here to speak about the ultimate purposes of human sexuality. It seems to me though that it was carefully designed to prepare human beings to find their fulfillment in someone beyond themselves and thus learn at the human level how we are supposed to relate to God. In the parent-child relationship in the home God intended us to learn to live with loving law and thus get ready to live with our heavenly Father. The human family is a parable and a preparation for life in the heavenly Father's home. In like manner the male-female relationship is a parable of our need of God, and marriage is both parable of and preparation for true communion with God in a love relationship that will never end. These two relationships were looked upon by God as extremely sacred. Violation of his pattern in either case brought the most serious consequences.

The other side of this is that only within these relationships will persons be fulfilled truly. To live at variance with God's way is really to live at variance with oneself. This means that from a biblical perspective homosexuality is not a condition that is original and true but developed and perverted. The development may have come very early in the person's life but it is not original. At the beginning, God made them male and female. Thus to be lenient on homosexuality, or condoning, is to encourage a person in the pursuit of a life against ultimate reality. It is encouraging a person to flee from himself. Homosexuality is thus a correctable condition. The God who made human beings originally can reconfirm them in their sexuality as he is able to reconfirm all fallen and perverted persons in holiness.

Thus the homosexual is not a special class of sinner that is the particular object of a special divine wrath. Homosexuals, like all of us, are the victims of sin and of a sinful society. God's grace is as available to them as to all the rest of this lost and blighted race. Rehabilitation may be difficult, but to suggest that there is fulfillment and salvation outside God's patterns is deceptive and cruel, perhaps eternally so. The business of the church then is, as Paul suggested in 2 Timothy 2:25, in meekness to instruct "those that oppose themselves."

NOTES

1. W. F. Arndt and F. W. Gingrich, trans. and eds., *A Greek-English Lexicon of the New Testament* (Chicago: University Press, 1957), pp. 489, 109.

2. D. S. Bailey, *Homosexuality and the Western Christian Tradition* (London: Longmann, Green, & Co., 1955), p. 40.

3. Troy Perry, "God Loves Me Too," in W. Dwight Oberholtzer, ed., *Is Gay Good?* (Philadelphia: Westminster Press, 1971). This work contains an extensive bibliography.

4. Bailey, *Homosexuality and the Western Christian Tradition,* pp. 41, 38.

5. John von Rohr, "Toward a Theology of Homosexuality," in Oberholtzer, ed., *Is Gay Good?*

6. Perry, "God Loves Me Too," pp. 119–20.

7. Ibid., pp. 116–20.

8. Bailey, *Homosexuality and the Western Christian Tradition,* p. 52.

9. Arndt and Gingrich, eds., *A Greek-English Lexicon of the New Testament,* p. 84.

10. Bailey, *Homosexuality and the Western Christian Tradition,* pp. 1–28.

11. Ibid., p. 15.

12. Ibid., p. 155.

13. Francis Brown, S. R. Driver, and Charles A. Briggs, eds., *A Hebrew and English Lexicon of the Old Testament,* based on the Lexicon of William Gesenius, 2nd ed. (Oxford: Clarendon Press, 1952).

SUGGESTED READING

Bergler, Inman. *Homosexuality: Disease or Way of Life?* New York: Collier Books, 1962.

Small, Dwight Hervey. *Christian, Celebrate Your Sexuality.* Old Tappan, NJ: Fleming H. Revell, 1974.

Thielicke, Helmut. *The Ethics of Sex.* Translated by John W. Doberstein. New York: Harper & Row, 1964.

8

The Church
and the Homosexual
Guy Charles

No other problem confronting the modern church is as multifaceted in its future implications as the relationship between the church and the homosexual. No denomination will be spared confrontation with the problem within the next few years. Already some denominations have given into the vocality of the Gay Liberationists,[1] and others are beginning to hear cries demanding equal rights from gay caucuses and task forces.[2] In this present church era of the social gospel we are beginning to subvert the salvific nature of the scriptural gospel for a humanistic approach to the problems of mankind. Because of the church's humanistic approach, Gay Liberationists are gaining ground in several areas: church support for gay civil rights legislation; ordination of homosexuals to the clergy; full approval of homosexuality by the church as a valid, healthy, normal, alternative life-style; and the ultimate sanction—gay marriages with

Guy Charles has been a designer for Broadway and TV, a commercial interior decorator, and an expert in copyright law and contracts publishing. Since his conversion to Christ, he has begun a counseling ministry to homosexuals with headquarters at Sanctuary House in Arlington, Virginia.

the adoption of children or granting custody to a gay parent at the time of divorce. Thus, the gay Christian family!

In order to recognize the problems and needs of the homosexual and the church, we must first strip ourselves of the fables, myths, and judgmental attitudes which have built up a "gay mystique" within our society. Homosexuality is not merely the sexual act between two persons of the same gender, male or female; it also encompasses the desires, the fantasies, the thoughts of the individual. It results from a process within rather than from physical attributes. It is the result of conditioning by the judgmental nature of other individuals and is not a birth defect or genetic heritage. It is an act of the will which, through continued practice, becomes a habit and eventually a life-style.

I make these statements as one who practiced homosexuality as a life-style and preference for more than thirty-seven years. I do not speak as a theologian, a biblical scholar, or a sociologist, or from medical, psychological, or psychiatric expertise. I have been a homosexual, have lived among homosexuals, and have been a leader in the Gay Liberation movement.

The Kinsey report of the '40s[3] is the basis for the estimated homosexual population of the United States. Gay Lib groups have utilized the Kinsey projections to estimate that there is a 10 percent minority of homosexuals within the general population, or in excess of twenty million. Though there are no official figures available, I doubt that the liberationists represent 10 percent of the entire homosexual community. Therefore we are being assailed with the cry "gay is good" by a few persons purporting to represent all homosexuals.

From my personal involvement in the homosexual world and from the content of thousands of letters our organization (Liberation) has received in the last two years, I am aware of the needs and struggles of these people. Most gay newspapers and magazines, such as the *Advocate* and *Gay Sunshine*, carry personal ads for contacts.

The ministry of Liberation has responded to more than ten thousand such ads, receiving approximately twenty-five hundred replies. Our original contact letter does not mention religion, Jesus Christ, or God, but asks if the person is tired of "bars, and baths, cruising public parks and restrooms, of placing ads for a lover."

Some of our contacts, just now replying after six months to a year, have kept our original letter. They ask to know about the joy and peace we have found and in which we live today. One seventeen-year-old states the case: "It's not gay, it's rotten. Only the young, the beautiful, and the strong survive. . . ."

The problem of homosexuality and the church is not limited to how the church can relate and minister to homosexuals in the outside world. Congregations have within their ranks those who have affirmed homosexual life-styles and are seeking companionship which allows them to retain both the life-style and their religion. The following excerpted ads demonstrate ways in which homosexuals are attempting to deal with these needs:

ANSWERED PRAYER, CHRISTIANS? Former Campus Crusade staff; gdlkg, masc., career-oriented Xtian . . . seeks same.

Very sincere Christian needs same to make a house into a home . . .

LOVE THE LORD? SO DO I. Evangelical, born-again guy, 27, looking for Christian companions.

And where does the church stand in relation to the homosexual who is seeking help, as well as the greater gay community? Those who wish to have equality at the expense of denying the true nature of the gospel would change the text of Scripture in meaning, context, and even language to support the cause of liberationists within and outside the church. They are willing to accept such terms as *affectional, sexual, orientation,* or *preference*[4] to be used interchangeably, not realizing that approving such designations may eventually allow such deviations as necrophilia, bestiality, and so on to become sanctions of the church. Such statements as, "We revere the inherent right of the individual to exercise free will in the making of moral and ethical decisions as well as freedom of conscience in the living of life . . . ,"[5] stated in relation to the previously noted terms strip the individual of any responsibility to God and release him from accountability in relationships with others.

The City Council of Washington, D.C., now has before it a proposal relating to a revision of the marriage and divorce laws.[6] The liberationists have succeeded in removing gender indications, thereby allowing the government to sanction marriage between two persons of the same sex. A member of the Human Rights Commission, a professed homosexual and one of the most vocal on all issues of gay liberation, testified that homosexuals must have this right of civil marriage. We are wondering where the denominational bodies who have passed resolutions regarding support of civil rights will stand when they are asked to solemnize gay marriages in their churches, especially when they reread the pronouncements and other statements of support which they have validated.

The churches must be wary in supporting liberationists and their demands for equal rights legislation. If the language of such statements of support is ambiguous, churches and denominations may unintentionally sanction a form of sexual activity and life-style antithetical to Christian belief and teaching. The effects of the "gay is good" propaganda of the activists,[7] as well as the tales of discrimination in civilian and military work forces, are already beginning to lull the church into a state of complacency. The loud voices of a few are being allowed to control the future of the majority.

Obviously many homosexuals experience loneliness, rejection, guilt, and fear and sincerely wish to change their sexual preference. The liberationists claim that these feelings will disappear once the homosexual is allowed the freedom to express his or her life-style without harm or injury to others.

On the other hand, there are those in the church whose continued use of passages from Scripture[8] condemning the sin of homosexuality blinds them to the saving nature of the gospel, and thereby they turn away the individual seeking help to overcome a homosexual life-style. It is primarily this group within the church which the gay task forces within many denominations wish to overcome. Unfortunately, they are winning the battle because of the complacency of the Bible-toters that comes from years of denying the homosexual the ability to approach God, once the homosexual's personal life-style has been made common knowledge.

Role-playing attitudes have incorrectly sought to categorize the attributes which make a man a man, and a woman a woman. We can thank the radical gay movements which began in the summer of 1969[9] for opening up the closet[10] doors to show us that effeminacy in the male and masculinity in the female do not preclude a heterosexual life-style. For example, the aggressive, sports-oriented male is susceptible to homosexuality, as well as the previously suspected retiring, artistic male. Age, profession, race, religious background, and so on must no longer be considered means of precluding homosexuality. If an extensive survey of the homosexual population were possible, we doubt if any two individuals would have identical histories which would show a determining cause of homosexuality.[11]

We also now have a newer problem within the church with the emergence of the charismatic phenomenon. Certain individuals claim that homosexuality is a demon or spirit[12] which must be exorcised in order for the individual to change his or her life-style. I feel sure that somewhere in the New Testament we would be given direct proof of such demon or spirit possession or infestation, by name, if such were the case. I have not come across it in ministering, but some do claim that their life-styles have been changed by exorcism.

In attempting to rationalize sin, instead of applying Christian morality, the church is becoming guilty of giving tacit approval to the climate of moral deviation in which the sensual or sexual person becomes more important than the spiritual being. The ministry of Liberation is directed toward helping the homosexually oriented individual, exclusively.

It is now time that the *entire* church returned to its obligation as the body of Christ to preach the gospel, minister in the truth of the Scripture, and thereby truly be able to call itself Christian. The definition of *Christian* is to believe in Jesus as the Christ and to follow his teachings.[13] When he was tempted in the desert, he stated, "It is written . . . It is written . . . It is written . . . ," defeating the temptations of the enemy (Matt. 4:4, 7; Luke 4:4, 8). He further stated that he came to fulfill the Law, not to destroy it (Matt. 5:17).

Yet we find ourselves listening to those within the church who would deny Scripture by stating that it was written for another day and age, not for modern or present usage. We hear some people declare that all before Jesus is void, for he gave us only one command, to love one another (John

13:34, 35; 15:12). In their humanistic approach to the Christian heritage of God's Word, they deny the infallibility of Scripture and thereby reduce the salvation of the Gospels, the hope of eternal life with God, to a mere existence on earth in this life. Do-gooders give everything to everyone whether it is in the best interests of the recipient or whether it might contribute to the person's moral debasement. Inherent in their view is the idea that there is no longer a judgment or price to be paid for sin.

What is the answer to ministering to the homosexual? Perhaps Paul Tournier best expresses the approach that is needed.

> As long as man is accused by the law, by society, by *other people*, he defends himself; it is a universal reflex. This defensive attitude prevents him from "coming to himself" and undergoing a moral experience. In the belief that it is leading him towards such an experience, society is in fact leading him away from it. But as soon as *other people*, instead of casting stones at him, recognize that in the perspective of the heart they are as guilty as he, he accuses *himself*, he repents and undergoes that moral experience which the Gospel calls salvation.[14]

In Romans, Paul reiterates Proverbs when he tells us to be kind to our enemy and thereby heap "coals of fire" upon him (see Rom. 12:20; Prov. 25:22). If we can accomplish this with an enemy, we can certainly succeed to a greater extent with those we love as brother and sister in the Lord. The Lord can convict them as we minister with the promises of the gospel, rather than with the condemnation of the Law.

The liberationists within the church continuously quote John 13:34 and the need to love one another; unfortunately they pervert the sense of the text to mean physical love. We as Christians have this commandment to act upon in ministering to the homosexual. In our work we find it one of the major resources from the Gospels to help the homosexual change his or her life-style. We ask a person to forget that *he* or *she* is committing a sin when about to commit a deviant sexual act. We ask him or her to think of the other person, whether a Christian or not, and to consider whether he or she will cause the other person to sin. By adding a responsibility for the other person, the counselee finds a satisfaction in *not* performing the act. Continued reference to responsibility for others encourages the individual to reverse an act of the will which eventually breaks the habit which has become a life-style.

This emphasis on responsibility is most effective if the individual is in a Christian leadership position as an or- dained minister or as a member of the laity. Yes, a growing number of leaders within the church have the problem of homosexuality and are in a position to corrupt the morality of those under their care. This is a fact which we cannot escape, and it poses a real problem to the future of the church. An article in *Campus Life* tells of a minister who was responsible for leading a high school group and, through his approaches to younger kids, turned others away from religion.[15] We mentioned the young man of seventeen who wrote. In the same letter he states that after accepting the Lord he joined a pentecostal church, where "the minister took an immediate 'liking' to me and I became his 'buddy.' Shortly after, he seduced me in the conference room. My first lover, with six kids yet. This relationship continued— all the while he told me you could be gay and a Christian too. (Funny how he kept reminding me to keep my mouth shut.) Then he got tired of me and I got dumped. (He was 45, I was 17.)"

When ordained ministers have the ability to turn others away from Jesus Christ, or the church, through their own selfish and lustful desires, we must carefully consider the ordination of self-proclaimed homosexuals. Yet these men are also redeemable. We contacted one pastor whose life-style followed that of the latter case mentioned. We explained that his desires for young boys were known and that he could find help if he so desired. He did, and through the matter of responsibility being put to him, he has been able to divest himself of homosexual desires.

We have become so accustomed to viewing homosexuality as a problem for the single person, and even then only in the male, that we overlook the broader aspects of the problem. In our ministry we are becoming increasingly aware of the number of homosexuals who are married, who have families, and whose sexuality and its appetite have diverted them from a heterosexual relationship with their spouse. More than 40 percent of our counselees fall into this category.

When a married person is involved in homosexual incidence, we must also look at the sexual relationship between the spouses. The responsibility for the marriage relationship, as well as for raising the family, can weigh heavily on husband or wife. If the burden is kept to oneself until a point of no communication exists, a relationship of self-interest may be sought with someone outside the marriage. When that outside relationship is homosexual, it is important to get the two spouses into a communicational relationship whereby the reasons for the extramarital affair can be discovered. When this is not accomplished, when an openness is not secured, the homosexual life, with its minimum of responsibility regarding family, becomes more and more attractive, and the individual will continue to seek it.

Fear is a primary emotional state in any relationship concerning homosexuality. The homosexual fears being exposed, a major barrier to assisting the individual to alter his or her life-style. The nonhomosexual fears what he does not understand about homosexuality; the individual who has homosexual fantasies fears succumbing to a gay life-style; church and society repress their fears by vocally condemning the homosexual individual rather than denouncing the life-style itself. When we are able to dispel these fears, we shall be able to minister to the homosexual with full power of the gospel. The Christian faith and message are not based on fear but on hope (see John 3:15, 16, 5:24, 6:47, 11:26; 1 John 5:11, 12, 13). This hope comes from the truth that is the Word of God. We must minister with that truth in order to give hope to the homosexual, and in that hope the joy and peace of soul which comes from a fulfilled life.

In ministering to the homosexual, we must keep that hope in mind. Although it is impossible to discuss the many variances in homosexual behavior and the particular needs in counseling each individual, we have discovered some effective guidelines which each and every Christian can utilize in a personal ministry to the homosexual, whether spouse, child, friend, or stranger.

1. Listen with an open mind to the homosexual who attempts to unburden his or her problem, regardless of the language or descriptions used.
2. Always remember that the homosexual is redeemable from his or her sexual life-style. If it was possible in the early church, it is possible now. The only requisite is a desire to change on the part of the individual.
3. You can build that desire within the individual by showing the love of Jesus Christ rather than the condemnation of man. In the face of such love, the individual will judge his or her life-style and find it lacking.
4. Do not quote Scripture verses which condemn the sin unless you're asked to name them. Rather, quote passages which proclaim deliverance from sin and promises of life and hope.

5. After a counseling relationship of trust has been established, get the individual to make a new commitment to Jesus Christ as his or her personal Savior.
6. Although the sexual desire for a homosexual life-style may be taken away immediately upon confession of guilt before God, this is not always the case. Remember that the individual is a spiritual child and must be helped to grow in the Christian walk. It may take a day, a week, a month, a year, or even two for a complete liberation from the life-style. You must continually be on hand for helpful counseling if the individual falls into old patterns.
7. Make sure that the individual forms Christian relationships within the church community and also that Bible study is included.
8. Remember, you are not accomplishing the miracle of liberation from the life-style; neither is the individual the means for his or her liberation other than through the desire for change. The Spirit of the living God begins the miracle in the spirit of the individual and defeats the desires of the senses, the flesh, and the sexual appetite through Jesus Christ.

In the foregoing I have used the term *homosexual* to represent both sexes, whether or not the individual is covert or overt in homosexual desires for sexual activity, fantasizing, thoughts, or relating to others. I prefer not to use the term *latent* for the covert homosexual since, in working with many individuals in the ministry, I have reached the conclusion that all individuals are born with genital sex but not with erotic desires. The awakening of the sexual drive comes through conditioning, education, and circumstance, as well as through the development of the bodily functions. This is why being homosexual is a choice of the will and not a genetic or hormonal imbalance or "gift of God" as many of the so-called gay churches and denominations would have us believe. Homosexuality is not contained in the sexual act alone. It can be a lust within the eye, the touch, or the mind. We must treat homosexuality from the biblical stance on adultery and fornication, which it really is, with the differentiation being in the sex of the two individuals concerned. In Matthew 5:28 we are told that lusting in the eye is the same as committing the sexual act.

This is an important fact for the counselor to remember. Unthinking gestures and remarks can lead a counselee to fantasize and fall back into the homosexual life-style. The counselor must always be aware of the possibility of a dependent relationship which can destroy the effectiveness of counseling. Age difference is no determinant in such situations. If the counselor is of peer age, the relationship can develop into one of a lover or mate. If there is a variance in age with the counselor being older, the effect can be a father relationship, and a son relationship if the counselor is younger. It is important for the counselor to reflect on the counseling session afterwards to make sure that the relationship is based on an unemotional level.

One does not need to be a charismatic, a fundamentalist, a liberal, or any other designation within the body of Christ to realize that we are living in an age of church history when false teachers, the self-desiring, and the apostates are becoming vocal within the church. The time that Paul described is already here: ". . . when people will not tolerate (endure) sound *and* wholesome instruction, but having ears itching [for something pleasing and gratifying], they will gather unto themselves one teacher after another to a considerable number chosen to satisfy their own liking *and* to foster the errors they hold, And will turn aside from hearing the truth and wander off into myths *and* man-made fictions" (2 Tim. 4:3, 4, Amplified Bible).

Homosexuality in the church, in each and every denomination, is going to be, and to some degree has already become, the issue on which all Christians must decide the question, Are we here to fulfill the commands and worship the Creator by the means he has given us in his Spirit, and his son Jesus Christ, or are we here to proclaim a god of our own humanism through the personal interpretation of human experience in the world? We are challenged to put aside our own likes and dislikes, fears, judgmental and condemnatory natures, and begin to assume the responsibility that comes with accepting the name Christian, the Christian faith, and above all Jesus Christ who told us: "Love one another; just as I have loved you, so you too should love one another. By this shall all [men] know you are My disciples, if you love one another—if you keep on showing love among yourselves" (John 13:34, 35, Amplified Bible).

The love he speaks about places the other individual before self, as he did; that "spiritual" love brings more souls into the body of Christ, for his glory, not ours. It does not condone sin as set down by God but brings liberation to the sinner through his love in us. This is the love the homosexual man or woman needs, desires, and must have if we as Christians are to bring all souls into salvation, to hope, to liberation from loneliness, rejection, fear, and guilt.

NOTES

1. The Tenth General Synod of the United Church of Christ (UCC) recently approved a pronouncement calling for support of equal rights for gays, as well as further studies. The American Lutheran church and American Baptists have also funded moves for study of gays in the church.
2. The following groups are now active: Dignity (Roman Catholic); Integrity (Episcopal); Lutherans Concerned; Gay

Presbyterians; task forces with the National Council of Churches, Methodists, Seventh-day Adventists, and the United Churches of Christ.

3. See A. C. Kinsey, W. B. Pomeroy, and C. Martin, *Sexual Behavior in the Human Male* (Philadelphia: W. B. Saunders, 1948); *Sexual Behavior in the Human Female* (Philadelphia: W. B. Saunders, 1953).

4. Terms taken from Intro. #554, a proposed amendment to the Administrative Code of the City of New York, before the New York City Council; and the Pronouncement on Civil Liberties without Discrimination related to Affectional or Sexual Preference, adopted by the Tenth General Synod of the United Churches of Christ.

5. From the UCC Pronouncement.

6. Bill No. 1–89 in the Council of the District of Columbia, introduced by Councilmember Arrington Dixon, 6 May 1975.

7. First introduced by Dr. Frank Kameny in his unsuccessful campaign for election as U.S. representative of the District of Columbia in 1970 and adopted by the Gay Movement nationally beginning in 1971.

8. The major verses used to condemn the sin of homosexuality are: Gen. 8:21, 13:13, 18:20, 19:1–28; Lev. 18:22, 26–29, 20:13; Deut. 29:21–25, 32:32, 33; Judg. 19; Rom. 1:18–32; 1 Cor. 6:9, 10.

9. Although there has been a growing activism in homophile organizations since the early 1940s with such organizations as SIR, Mattachine, and Daughters of Bilitis, the radical Gay Movement traces its beginnings to the "Stonewall Incident" of June 29, 1969, when police raided a homosexual bar in Greenwich Village in New York for violation of various city codes. Patrons of the bar were aided by members of antiwar groups in the village to fight back the police action with bricks, stones, fists, and arson, which continued throughout the weekend. Soon after, the Gay Liberation Front cells were formed which were the first Gay Lib organizations.

10. In gay slang *closet* is someone who is homosexual but who is afraid of his or her sexual life-style being known, or someone who has homosexual tendencies or fantasies but is afraid to act upon them to the point of sexual encounter.

11. The studies that have been conducted thus far have not been representative of the homosexual population in relation to the general population. The studies have either used a limited

number of cases or have been too specific in their approach.

12. See Frank and Ida Mae Hammond, *Pigs in the Parlor* (Impac Books).

13. *Webster's New World Dictionary of the American Language*, 2d college ed. (Cleveland, Ohio: World Publishing, 1970).

14. Paul Tournier, *The Person Reborn* (New York: Harper & Row, 1966).

15. Gary Fagan, "I Will Still Follow Jesus," *Campus Life*, February 1975.

9

Sex Education
in the Home
Letha Scanzoni

During the reign of the emperor Nero, a writer named
Petronius composed a classic comedy satirizing the man-
ners and morals of Rome. Had books been assigned ratings
in the fashion of the modern motion picture industry,
Petronius's book, *The Satyricon,* would have received at least
an R rating—quite possibly an X. The story is explicit on
sexual matters, and the author didn't hesitate to use the
Latin equivalent of four-letter words!

One scene in *The Satyricon* can provide a lesson for
parents and all others entrusted with the sex education of
children and teenagers. A husband and wife were deeply
concerned about their son and wanted to shield him from
sexual temptations—especially homosexual ones. Thus they
placed the boy in the care of a man who had taken lodging
in their home and who had impressed them with his evident
aversion to homosexual practices, a man who later boasted
that he had pretended to be scandalized at the mere mention of the topic. There is no evidence that the parents provided the boy with any understanding of sex; they felt that
his best protection from both knowledge and experience in
sexual matters would lie in having a constant chaperone.

The man could be the young boy's moral tutor, adviser, and supervisor of studies, staying with him day and night, and keeping him from any possibility of seduction. Of course, as you've probably guessed, the tutor himself took advantage of the boy's innocence and through a series of clever tricks and bribes introduced him to the very experiences from which the boy's parents had hoped to shield him.[1]

The point of this illustration for our purposes is not that the incident involved homosexual acts; it could just as easily have been a story of a young girl seduced by a man or a young boy introduced to sex by a woman. Indeed, such was the case with the legendary Don Juan, who was seduced at age sixteen. Byron's epic poem, *Don Juan*, tells of the boy's ultraprudish mother who hired learned tutors to make sure "that his breeding should be strictly moral" and required that all studies first be submitted to her so that she could exercise censorship on anything bordering on the sexual side of life. Yet, Don Juan learned on his own and in adolescence embarked on the life of sexual looseness which is conjured up in our minds by the very mention of his name.[2]

I'm also reminded of a boy in my neighborhood during my own childhood. He lived with his mother and grandmother. These women were so determined that this twelve-year-old boy should be spared the experience of coming into contact with anything sexual that they went through every magazine that came into the home and clipped out any hint of sex or nudity. Only then was the boy permitted to read the magazines. I've often wondered whatever became of him.

I think too of the angry mother who recently wrote to one of the major television networks protesting the use of the word *virgin* on one of their programs. The woman's young daughter had watched the program and asked what the word meant. The mother was quite upset at the question and complained to network officials that letting such material go out over the air made things extremely difficult for parents who were then called upon to do a lot of explaining to their children! Evidently, it never occurred to that mother that her child's question provided an excellent opportunity for sex education. There are other similar illustrations of parents who thought they could help their children best by sheltering them from knowledge of sex. One father took his children out of Sunday school when he heard that a lesson made mention of circumcision. A mother was shocked when her daughter excitedly told of a film she had seen at school. It showed how a baby forms from a tiny ovum within the mother. "Just think, *I* was once a little egg like that!" exclaimed the girl. But the mother's reaction was one of dismay, and she began phoning neighbors to start a campaign to take sex education classes out of the school. (A sidelight on this story, incidentally, is that this child, who had been on her way to a positive, wholesome outlook on sex, ceased to share her feelings with her mother. During her high-school years, the girl became pregnant and dropped out of school to get married.)

All of these parents were well intentioned. However, when we try to shield youngsters from sexual knowledge, we are actually failing them. What we do in such a case (not deliberately, of course) is to hand them over to other sources of information—young friends who may also be poorly informed, movies, magazines picked up at the newsstand, and so on. How much better that we ourselves as Christian parents provide them with the information they need—guidance that can be given in the context of a vital faith in God and undergirded by the teachings of his Word! Our sons and daughters do not need sheltering and protection so much as they need to learn how to handle and cope with the sexual openness of today's society.

This brings us to the second reason that I chose to begin

with Petronius's sexually explicit satire on the society of imperial Rome. It's important to see how mistaken are notions that children in our day are exposed to the topic of sex to a greater degree than at any previous time in history. There is simply no basis for a nostalgic longing for some imaginary "good old days" when rearing children was easy and sex-related questions, problems, and temptations never arose. Never has there been such a time. Petronius was writing his *Satyricon* at the very time that many of the New Testament Epistles were being written. In other words, this was what life was like in the long-ago world of Bible times, and yet God expected his people to live up to his standards and to train their children likewise. That's why Paul wrote to the Thessalonian Christians: "This is the will of God, that you should be holy: you must abstain from fornication; each one of you must learn to gain mastery over his body, to hallow and honour it, not giving way to lust like the pagans who are ignorant of God" (1 Thess. 4:3–5, NEB).

To go back even further in time, think of the old Testament world. The ancient Israelites were surrounded by nations of idol worshipers whose liturgy centered around fertility cult practices. At that time people of the Near East felt that productivity of fields, animals, and people depended on the goodwill of fertility gods and goddesses. In honor of these deities who were thought to control reproduction, ritualistic sexual orgies were held. Temples employed prostitutes, and sex acts were part of the religious ceremonies held therein. Images of the male and female genitals were publicly displayed for purposes of idol worship. Small clay figurines of nude pregnant women were carried about, possibly for home worship. Yet, in such a setting, God said: "You shall love the Lord your God with all your heart, and with all your soul, and with all your might. And these words which I command you this day

shall be upon your heart; and you shall teach them diligently to your children, and shall talk of them when you
sit in your house, and when you walk by the way, and when
you lie down, and when you rise. . . . You shall not go
after other gods, of the gods of the people who are round
about you; for the Lord your God in the midst of you is a
jealous God" (Deut. 6:5–7, 14–15, RSV). Children were to
learn to reject the sexual idolatry and values of the people
round about at the same time that they were to learn
obedience and loyalty to the Lord God *in their midst*. I
believe God is saying the same thing to us today, again
backed up by the promises of his presence and power. It is
not a matter of shielding and protecting our children or trying to hide our heads in the sand or run away from the kind
of emphasis on sex we sometimes see in today's world. We
need to face life as it is, not with fear but with confidence,
believing that God wants to answer the prayer of Jesus: "I
pray not that thou shouldest take them out of the world, but
that thou shouldest keep them from the evil" (John 17:15).

A LOOK AT THE WORLD

The term *world* is used here in the sense of the climate
of the times. If we are to give our children adequate sex
education, we must know something of the world in which
they are growing up. What are the sexual values being presented by the mass media? To what extent is sexual activity
outside of marriage taking place? What kinds of questions
about sex are being raised?

A book for physicians suggests that they see some of the
erotic films and read some of the sexually explicit books
available today in order to become better counselors by
understanding the milieu in which young persons are growing up.[3] I think that's wise advice for parents, pastors, and
other counselors, too. Those who don't wish to see the films

or read the books should at least have some idea of their contents through reading reviews. We need to prepare ourselves to help our children develop discernment with regard to materials to which they are exposed in these times. Especially do we need to guide them so that they can learn to view matters from a distinctly Christian perspective.

Second, we need to be aware of research findings. To keep abreast of new information, it is a good idea to check with the local library or subscribe to periodicals that report the research and discoveries of behavioral scientists in easily understood terms. *Human Behavior, Psychology Today, Society,* or *Family Planning Perspectives* (published by the Planned Parenthood Federation of America) are examples of journals that might be consulted. University libraries would have the first-hand reports of major studies in the professional journals of the behavioral sciences.

A study by two social scientists from Johns Hopkins University based upon a national representative sample of over four thousand never-married young women aged fifteen to nineteen years revealed that nearly three out of ten young women in this age group were no longer virgins.[4] Boys were not included in this particular study, but from the Kinsey surveys and other studies, there is good reason to believe that the percentage of sexually experienced young males may be even higher.

One of the most striking findings of this research was that sexual activity is beginning at younger ages. If premarital intercourse is increasing among teenagers, Christian parents have all the more reason to provide a good, sound sex education long before their youngsters reach the adolescent years. From early childhood, girls and boys should be carefully instructed in the two main aspects of sex education: the facts about human sexuality and moral guidance. Otherwise, they may not be prepared for the peer pressures and tempting situations that may arise even in the early teens, and they can easily be taken off-guard. "You get pressures put on you from both sides," one high school student told me, "from those who say 'do' and those who say 'don't.' How can you know what to do?" Another Christian high schooler wrote: "I worry many times about what the Lord thinks of just how far you should go with your boyfriend or girlfriend. Just how far is too far? And if it *is* too far, how do you say no?"

Such comments and questions bring us to another area we must be aware of in understanding the climate of the times—the rethinking that is going on about sexual attitudes and behavior. For example, some young people feel that sexual intercourse should be reserved for marriage but that any other sexual behavior is permissible beforehand. Thus, petting practices are widespread—including such intimate forms as breast and genital contact and petting to orgasm. In my book, *Sex Is a Parent Affair*, I've tried to provide some guidelines for parents and teenagers in thinking through this subject in a Christian perspective.[5]

We should also be aware of two principal outlooks on sex that are espoused by many today. One ethic is based on *hedonism* and emphasizes a pleasure-centered approach to sex. This is the *Playboy* view. Sex is fun, and that's really all that matters. The other sex ethic is based on *humanism*. Whereas hedonism is pleasure-centered, humanism is person-centered. In this view, if two persons are relating to each other as whole persons and are not exploiting each other but simply want to express their love, then sexual intercourse could be all right in their particular circumstances— even though they aren't married to each other. Christian parents and leaders need to be prepared to answer the arguments for this second view in particular, because I find in traveling around the country speaking to high school and college men and women that a significant number of Christian young people are taking it very seriously.

Out of concern for such young adults I devoted a great deal of study to finding out the basic principles of sex ethics that are provided in the Bible and tried to put together a way of answering some of the new questions that have been raised in recent years. The result of these efforts was the book, *Sex and the Single Eye,* now published under the title, *Why Wait? A Christian View of Premarital Sex.*[6] I think we have to help young people understand what God's plan for marriage is and how sex fits into that plan. I think we also have to make clear that a Christian position on premarital sex includes appreciation for the humanist concern for full personhood and avoiding exploitation of persons, but that we go beyond that to a kind of *Christian* humanism—a position that stresses not only loving our neighbor as ourselves so that we want no hurt to come to the neighbor but rather goes beyond that to the first great commandment which emphasizes first loving God with all our heart, soul, and mind (Matt. 22:36–40). We are primarily accountable to God.

Another important consideration in dealing with the climate of openness in today's world is a realization of the many sex education opportunities that come our way simply through the television set and newspapers and magazines. Children old enough to ask questions about what they see and read should be given answers. In our home over the years, the mass media presentations of sexual subjects have stimulated many fascinating discussions with our sons on such topics as transsexual surgery, prostitution, homosexuality, living together outside of marriage, abortion, venereal diseases, rape, childbirth, nude bathing—to mention just a few of the topics that have come up recently. By taking advantage of the opportunities provided by what our children see and read and wonder about, we can prepare them for many of the questions and decisions about sex they will face later.[7]

The Bible is never squeamish about sex. It is frank and forthright in its discussions and has far more to say on the subject than most people realize. First, it's important that our children grasp something of the wonder of it all—the beauty, the goodness, the tremendous ecstasy associated with sex as God intended it. And then it's important that we help them understand the warnings of how sex may be misused and abused. Both kinds of messages are found in abundance in Scripture.

The wonder of sex in God's plan. The foundation for sex education lies in the story of creation in Genesis 1 and 2. Even while they are yet toddlers, children can be taught that God made us and God loves us. Young children can learn that God had a special plan in making the world and all the creatures he put within it. And then he made people to live in that world and enjoy it, people who could love him and praise him and talk with him, people who could be God's friends. Children can learn how wonderful God's design of the human body is (the way our eyes and ears work, the way babies grow, the way cuts heal, and so on), and they can learn Bible verses praising God for how he has made us (for example, Ps. 119:73; 139:13–14) or make up their own little songs or prayers thanking God for each part of their bodies.

We can help our children see that God made two different kinds of bodies for people—male bodies and female bodies. While there are many ways in which all our bodies are alike (eyes, ears, how we digest food, how we grow, how we breathe, and so on), there are some ways in which male bodies and female bodies are different. Parents and children can talk about some of these differences—how men's voices are low and women's are higher pitched, how women have breasts, how hair grows on men's faces, for example. God has also created special *parts* of the body that are different in males and females. God has designed the bodies of women and men so that they can fit together in a special way; God planned that in this way husbands and wives could have babies.

These are some of the points that children can learn gradually—not all at once, but in building-block fashion as parents are alert to questions and curiosity at different ages—and then build onto the foundation of wonder and joy in God's creation. Parents can talk about these matters in a natural fashion all day long while walking with their children, while observing animals and birds, or while reading Bible stories together. For example, try to get the children to talk about why God told Noah to put a male and female of each animal in the ark.

Children growing up in a Christian home can also learn from Genesis that God considered all he had made to be *very good.* They can be helped to see that sex is beautiful and good as God intended it; it is not something to be ashamed of or afraid of. No parts of our bodies are "dirty" or "bad." God made our bodies, every part, and what he made is very good.

As parents study the Scriptures and learn to see how an experience of what I like to call *joyous sexuality* is part of God's intention for marriage, they can become comfortable with their own feelings about sex and be better able to convey the scriptural sense of wonder to children approaching adolescence. Passages like the Song of Solomon and Proverbs 5:18–19 emphasize the utter delight in one another and the joy and playfulness of the marital embrace as husband and wife express their love physically. First Corinthians 7:3–4 speaks of the equality of the sexual relationship and recognizes that both women and men have sexual desires and both partners in a marriage have a responsibility to meet the sexual needs of the other. These are topics about which there is a great deal of discussion today, and parents can help their teenagers especially to see that the Bible addresses itself to these matters (including female sexuality) quite clearly.[8]

Warnings about misusing God's good gift of sex. When our older son was five or six years old, we were teaching him the Ten Commandments and were recasting some of them in simple language so that he would not simply memorize them but understand them. We were rather stumped, however, by the challenge of putting the commandment, "Thou shalt not commit adultery," into language that would be clearly understood by a young child. One children's book suggested, "Thou shalt think pure thoughts." But we felt that was in many ways more confusing than helpful and didn't really get across the meaning of the commandment. So we decided to recast it in the positive: "You shall want to please God in marriage." We explained that God wants husbands and wives to love each other in a very special way and to be faithful to each other. Steve made a little scrapbook and drew pictures to illustrate each commandment, and for that one he drew a bride and groom with Jesus performing the ceremony at the wedding. A few years later when he went with us to see the movie *Dr. Zhivago,* he said as we walked out, "That man had a wife and yet he went to that other woman's house and slept with her." We said, "Yes, and do you know which of God's commandments he was breaking?" Steve replied immediately, "The seventh one—the one about pleasing God in marriage." We asked if he knew what the man's behavior was called, and Steve was able to answer, "Adultery."

Children need to be helped in learning that God's warnings are for our good, a point emphasized in instructions to parents in Deuteronomy 6:24. A thumbnail sketch of the Bible's teachings on sexuality is found in Hebrews 13:4

where we are told that marriage is something good and honorable and that sex is a wonderful, important part of marriage; but at the same time, God will judge those who engage in fornication (sexual intercourse by unmarried persons) and adultery (a married person's taking part in sex relations with someone other than his or her spouse). This passage is a combination of the positive and the negative, and we must keep the two in balance. We must also make sure that children don't get the idea that sexual sins are the worst kinds of sins (Christians have given this impression all too often!), and we must also make clear God's forgiveness of those who have not obeyed his commandments but who are sorry and tell him so.

Some of the Scripture passages that are helpful in warning us about sexual sins and helping us to want God's way are found in 1 Thessalonians 4, 1 Corinthians 6:12–20 where we are told that the Christian's body is a temple of the Holy Spirit, and Romans 12:1, 2 where we are told to present our bodies to the Lord as living sacrifices. Parents may also find it beneficial to compare Deuteronomy 6 with Proverbs 6:20ff. In Deuteronomy the father and mother were told to provide information and instruction about God all day long in the everyday happenings of life, with God's commandments bound around their necks and in their hearts and similarly passed on to their children. The passage in Proverbs takes up where Deuteronomy leaves off. Now the young persons are themselves to have God's Word (as presented by their parents) bound upon their own hearts so that the commandments of God will guide them as they walk, talk, sleep, and go through the normal course of everyday life. Their parents' beliefs and values, based upon the Word of God, have now become their own beliefs and values. Behavioral scientists would say they have *internalized* what they were taught as children so that their attitudes and actions will be guided by their own convictions and not imposed by external sanctions. What's especially interesting about the Proverbs passage in this connection is that it goes on to show the young person that this personal commitment to God and what he has said is the way to keep from straying into a wrong use of God's good gift of sex.

We must convey to our children that a Christian position on sex ethics is not hedonistic (although joy in sex is recognized, but pleasure cannot be worshiped as an end in itself), nor is it humanistic (because this view doesn't go quite far enough, being concerned only with human-to-human relationships and not human-to-God responsibility). But in saying that Christian sex ethics go deeper than being pleasure-centered or even person-centered, I don't want to give the impression that the Christian's ethical standards are rule-centered—a confining list of dos and don'ts that take all the fun out of life. Rather, Christian sex ethics are Christ-centered. We belong to our Lord and want to please him in our sex life as well as in all other areas of life, knowing that only then can we experience life at its best—life abundant—and true sexual freedom.[9]

A LOOK AT THE WORKS OF GOD

The design of the human body is marvelous. No wonder the psalmist cried: "O Lord, how manifold are thy works! In wisdom hast thou made them all" (Ps. 104:24, RSV) and "Great are the works of the Lord, studied by all who have pleasure in them" (Ps. 111:2, RSV). If we really have pleasure in the Lord and his works, we'll want to be studying them, learning all we can about how he has made us. If parents are going to do a good job of sex education in the home, they should be applying themselves to studying for themselves the male and female reproductive systems and preparing in advance for their children's questions. Many materials are available today to help us in this task; I've listed many of them in a special section of *Sex Is a Parent Affair,* and there are new books coming out all the time. Good teachers know their subjects, and that means study on the teacher's part. Parents who want to be good sex educators should be as thoroughly acquainted with their subject as possible, including knowing the correct names for the various parts of the body and being able to explain how they work, what their functions are, and so on.

It's important to keep the climate of the home warm and open so that children feel loved and accepted (the experience of human love and cuddling is the first lesson in sex education). In such an atmosphere children feel free to talk about sexual topics without fear of being told, "You're too young to know about that," or "Where did you ever hear such a nasty word!" These kinds of evasions and shocked reactions from parents cut off communication and serve no good purpose in sex education.

It's a good idea for parents to think through in advance how they would answer certain questions should they come up; that way they won't be caught unprepared. If a child does want to discuss something the parent hadn't anticipated, the parent can simply admit that he or she has wondered about that, too, and suggest they look up the information together. If parents can learn to relax and talk about sex in a natural manner, building upon all they have taught the child over the years about the Creator's wonderful works, there shouldn't be any trouble in conveying both accurate information and good attitudes. In this regard, I'd like to close with an excerpt from *Sex Is a Parent Affair:*

> Many parents are able to answer the earliest questions about reproduction without embarrassment. It isn't too hard to say that a baby grows inside a special place God made in a mother's body, or that the baby began as a wee, tiny egg that was joined by a special sperm cell, or even that the sperm cell

came from the daddy's body. But it's the anticipation of the big question—"How does the daddy put the sperm cell in the mommy?"—that makes parents nervous, flustered and tongue-tied.

Such fears and nervousness should not be necessary. If a child is old enough to ask about sex, he or she is old enough to be told the truth. Simply explain that God has designed the father's body so that sperm cells are made in a little bag of skin that hangs between his legs. God has also designed the father's penis so that it will fit into a special opening in the mother's body—the vagina. Because a husband and wife love each other, they want to be as close together as possible. God designed their bodies to fit together just perfectly. At special times as they lie together in bed, a husband and wife show their love for each other by joining together. The father places his penis into the mother's vagina. Sperm cells pass through his penis into the vagina, and then swim up into the uterus and tubes, where they may meet a tiny egg cell. If a sperm joins with an egg, a baby begins to grow inside the wife. When a husband and wife show their love in this special way, it's called "sexual intercourse," or "sex relations."

God's design of male and female bodies to fit together this way is really very marvelous and nothing to be ashamed of. . . . Of course, sexual intercourse is more than "fitting together." And it's also more than procreation. Some children have the impression that husbands and wives have sex relations only in connection with having a baby. Thus a child may tell a friend, "My parents did it three times. Yours must have done it twice because you only have one sister." The procreative side of sex is important and more easily understood by children. But school-age children can also begin understanding that there is an emotional-pleasurable-communicative side to sexual intercourse.

At the appropriate time you can explain that husbands and wives like to show their love in this special way. Perhaps you can say, "You know how you like that happy, warm feeling of being cuddled and told we love you? Look how many times you say, 'Hug me, Mommy!' or 'Squeeze me real tight, Daddy.' Well, it's something like that with a husband and wife. They love each other very, very much. They like to hug and kiss and be very close to each other. God made their bodies in a special way so that they can be so close it's like being one person—because that's what God says being married is supposed to be like. Although married couples show their love in lots of other ways, God planned sexual intercourse as a very *special* way of showing their oneness.[10]

This, then, is one way we can handle sex questions in light of our Christian faith. It is a way of helping our youngsters "know that the Lord is God! It is he that made us, and we are his" (Ps. 100:3, RSV). What God has made is very good and is to be accepted with thanksgiving and joy.

Sex education in the home is a privilege and a challenge. May God help us to creatively take hold of that privilege and respond to that challenge because we love him and because we love our children.

NOTES

1. Petronius, *The Satyricon*, trans. William Arrowsmith (New York: New American Library, Mentor Books, 1959), pp. 90–91.

2. For a discussion of Byron's point that morality is not a matter of prudish sheltering, see Virginia Ramey Mollenkott, *Adamant and Stone Chips: A Christian Humanist Approach to Knowledge* (Waco, Tex.: Word Books, 1967), pp. 46–47.

3. William A. Daniel, Jr., M.D., *The Adolescent Patient* (St. Louis: C. V. Mosby Co., 1970), p. 75.

4. John F. Kantner and Melvin Zelnik, "Sexual Experience of Young Unmarried Women in the United States," *Family Planning Perspectives* 4 (October 1972), pp. 9–18.

5. Letha Scanzoni, *Sex Is a Parent Affair: Help for Parents in Teaching Their Children about Sex* (Glendale, Cal.: G/L Regal Books, 1973), pp. 212–18.

6. Letha Scanzoni, *Why Wait? A Christian View of Premarital Sex* (Grand Rapids, Mich.: Baker Book House, 1975).

7. In *Sex Is a Parent Affair*, I have included a section entitled "What If a Child Asks about . . . ?" in which twenty-five sex-

related topics are discussed (e.g., abortion, masturbation, pornography, homosexuality, sex slang) and suggestions are made for talking over each subject with children in three age categories: preschool, school age, and adolescence.

8. Scanzoni, *Sex Is a Parent Affair*, chaps. 1, 2.

9. Scanzoni, *Why Wait?*, chap. 9.

10. Scanzoni, *Sex Is a Parent Affair*, pp. 233–35. Reprinted by permission of G/L Publications, Glendale, CA 91209. © copyright 1973 by G/L Publications.

10

Sex,
Inside and Outside Marriage
David A. Seamands

The subject of this chapter encompasses a vast number of specific topics, all of which cannot be adequately covered in a limited number of pages. I will limit discussion therefore to the more general and familiar aspects of sexual activity inside and outside marriage. I shall consider these from a Christian perspective and relate them, not only to us as individual Christians, but also to the family. Christian parents have a special responsibility to seek better ways of guiding children to the deepest understanding and highest fulfillment of their sexuality.

A CHRISTIAN PHILOSOPHY OF SEX

A Christian philosophy of sex is based on the view of human personhood which emerges from the biblical account of creation.[1] According to Genesis 1 and 2, God's crowning act of creation was making mankind (generic, not man the

David A. Seamands is pastor of the Wilmore United Methodist Church, host church to Asbury College and Asbury Theological Seminary, in Wilmore, Kentucky. He and his wife, Helen, are active leaders in the Marriage Enrichment Program. They have three grown children.

male). Formed from the dust of the ground but made in his own likeness, "in the image of God he created him; male and female he created them" (Gen. 1:27, RSV). Thus we humans are rooted in nature and share this in common with all other created beings. We are part chemical, mineral, vegetable, and animal. But we are more, for though related to and rooted in nature we are also related to and rooted in the very nature of the triune God. This is the basis of our social and spiritual nature. We transcend all other created beings. Only humans can stand in self-conscious relationship with their Creator and with one another.

Sexuality is an essential part of our personal identity; maleness and femaleness are intrinsic to the image of God in human nature. One cannot think of a normal person (including oneself) without thinking of "he" or "she." However, this masculinity or femininity is not complete within itself. A divine discontent has been built into it: "Then the *Lord God* said, 'It is not good that the man should be *alone*'" (Gen. 2:18, RSV, italics mine). Each sex requires the other for completion and fulfillment. The attraction and pull toward the opposite sex is more than mere biological urge; it is profoundly social and spiritual as well. It is indeed evidence of the deep desire of the total person for wholeness and completeness.

Thus rooted in man's essential nature (dust and divine) sex is partly chemical and mineral; it is affected by hormones and glands and related to certain areas and organs of the body. Sex is also partly animal; humans share with many warm-blooded mammals a number of similar sexual activities. But sex is much more than that. Certain divinely created differences lift it to the spiritual plane. Animal sex is purely seasonal, glandular, instinctual, and compulsive. Human sex is mind controlled and under the direction of the will and the spirit. This is why it has been said that the chief sex organ is the brain. Human sex is, above all, relational and can become sacramental, "the outward and visible sign of an inward and spiritual bond uniting" two persons. Men and women are the only creatures able to have sexual relations face to face. Sex is communication and union in its highest and most intimate form. It is communion of body, mind, emotions, and spirit—the total person. It is *psycho-soma-pneumatic* union: ". . . and the two shall become one" (Eph. 5:31, RSV).

The most ecstatic and fulfilling expression of this union is the one-flesh sexual relationship of a husband and wife within marriage. Indeed God has clearly limited sex in its highest form to the confines of marriage. Its very total commitment nature demands the covenant relationship of marriage. Thus the restrictions and commandments of Scripture which surround sex are not to lessen its enjoyment. Rather they are God's way of enabling us to use this great gift, perhaps the greatest of all his gifts, for our fullest enjoyment and our highest fulfillment.

SEX BEFORE MARRIAGE

Masturbation. Although Menninger states that the taboo against masturbation vanished almost overnight at the turn of this century,[2] the taboo about discussing it certainly did not. In spite of the fact that it is perhaps the most widely engaged-in sexual activity, it is rarely talked about. Nearly everybody does it, but nobody talks about it. Only in the past few decades have secular sources begun to write about it, while up-to-date Christian discussion has been limited to recent years.[3] Secular psychologists and psychiatrists tend to confuse the issue by making the term too inclusive;[4] so a simple definition is in order.

Masturbation is deliberate and conscious self-stimulation so as to produce sexual excitement with the goal of orgasm. Whether or not the goal is achieved depends upon age and other factors, but it is certainly the ultimate aim of the sexual arousal. Masturbation can be observed in small children, but the chief period for it is during adolescence and early young adulthood. Without doubt it is the major sexual activity of teenagers.

William Hulme quotes the old joke, "Ninety-nine out of a hundred teen-age boys and girls masturbate and the other one's a liar."[5] Just how widespread is it? For obvious reasons it is not possible to state with complete accuracy, but data derived from questioning thousands of people in clinical surveys leaves no doubt that it is an extremely common practice among both males and females of all ages. The Sex Information and Education Council of the United States (SIECUS) says that about 90 percent for males and above 60 percent for females, over a period of time, is a realistic figure.[6] Most experienced counselors would confirm similarly high percentages on the basis of their own records.

What should be the Christian attitude toward such a common practice? In the past it has been totally, almost violently, condemned without any open and adequate reasons given. Jack Wyrtzen's book on youth's purity problems is typical: ". . . secret sins. You know what I'm talking about—I don't have to spell it out; those vile, dirty personal pollutions."[7] One writer states he has seen a large roomful of university men praying for forgiveness and strength to resist this sin.[8] With such a high percentage of active incidence among youth, how can any evangelist fail to fill the counseling room or altar when he cries out against "secret sins" or "lust in solitude"?

Modern evangelical Christian writers and counselors vary greatly in their attitude toward masturbation. J. E. Adams, in a chapter entitled "Masturbation Is Sin,"[9] condemns it *in toto* because of its enslaving nature and lustful thoughts. He says it is a perversion of the sexual act which is not presented as an option in the Bible. T. J. Bingham declares that masturbation is an evil but not wholly evil since it is a sin without the social consequences of other sexual sins.[10] H. J. Miles has a detailed, thorough, and excellent examination of the subject, discussing when masturbation is sinful and when it is not.[11] M. O. Vincent points out it is one of those gray areas for Christians and that each incident has to be treated individually. He comes out fairly close to Miles's conclusion.[12] William Hulme takes a similar position and seems to treat masturbation as more immature than sinful.[13] Charlie Shedd takes some of the above arguments and carries them further, saying that there are times when masturbation can be regarded as a gift from God and a wise provision for growing up.[14]

Let me now set forth my own conclusions on the subject, which are based on counseling uncountable numbers of people.

There is no clear and direct word on masturbation anywhere in Scripture. The two passages used in ancient times, Genesis 38:8–11 and 1 Corinthians 6:9, 10 have nothing to do with it. Onan's sin was his failure to obey the ancient Hebrew law by practicing *coitus interruptus* and was not masturbation. The King James Version term "abusers of themselves," in the Corinthian list, was a mistranslation and is now correctly rendered "homosexuals" in all modern versions.

When we know how almost universal and ancient masturbation is (it is mentioned in the *Egyptian Book of the Dead,* circa 1550–950 B.C.)[15] and when every other sexual sin such as fornication, adultery, homosexuality, and bestiality are listed and clearly condemned, why is it—if it is always a sin —nowhere mentioned in the Bible? I realize the argument from silence is dangerous, but in the case of something so widespread and well known it would seem to be conspicuous by its absence.

From a scientific and medical standpoint we now know

that there is no mental or physical harm in masturbating; so there are no moral arguments for health reasons. All this means that we will have to use other related Christian principles in determining its rightness or wrongness.

I believe the act of masturbation in itself is neither good nor evil. Two basic Christian principles determine this. First, *the thought life.* When masturbation is accompanied by sexual fantasies, it clearly comes under the condemnation of Christ's words about "mental adultery" in Matthew 5:27, 28 and is a sin. According to SIECUS, masturbation is usually accompanied by such fantasies in three-fourths of all males who masturbate and half of all females.[16] However, I agree with Miles that the experience is possible without fantasy or lust; so it cannot simply be taken for granted that it is always a lustful and thus a sinful act.

Second, *the social and relational life.* When masturbation, with or without lust, becomes an emotional substitute for proper interpersonal relationships, when it is used as a means of escaping from the pressures of loneliness, frustration, and depression, then there is no question that it is harmful to the person and therefore wrong from a Christian viewpoint.

Years of counseling have forced me to distinguish between masturbation as a temporary and occasional means of relieving normal sexual build-up (almost an inevitable part of normal growing up, particularly for teen-age boys) and masturbation as a compulsive enslaving habit which feeds, and is in turn fed by, deeper emotional hang-ups. Some of these would include an inability to relate to any person—especially those of the opposite sex—depression, deep-seated resentments, and the inability to find normal ways of coping with frustration and anxiety. In this case masturbation is really only a symptom for deeper problems which are far more serious and damaging than it is. In my experience some of the worst cases of the latter kind are among married persons. Masturbation can, in a Christian, unfortunately become the peg upon which he hangs his guilts and anxieties that keep him from actually getting to the real problem. Parents, pastors, and Christian counselors must learn to discern the difference between the various types.

I have discovered the following to be some practical ways of dealing with masturbation:

(1) Do not try a direct, frontal spiritual attack. Instead of lessening the problem, it usually makes it worse. Nothing provokes masturbation more than to create anxiety about it. Try to get the person's mind off his guilt and anxiety by explaining to him that it is one of those gray areas where rightness or wrongness depends on other factors. Usually he has already tried prayer and Scripture reading with the only result that he feels worse than ever for breaking his promises to God. His prayers are often doing more harm than good, for they are totally negative. Words of reassurance about God's accepting love, his faithfulness even when we fail, and teaching the person how to pray positively ("Thank you, Lord, for loving me and healing me and helping me with all my problems") will break the vicious circle of guilt and despair.

(2) Get his mind onto his social life and his interpersonal relationships. Often he is a lone wolf and needs to break out of himself. "Socialize, don't fantasize" is another good suggestion. Persons who do this find within a matter of a few months that the compulsive nature of masturbation has been broken, reduced to a minor and only occasional means of relieving sexual tensions which finally may be abandoned altogether. The true joys of making friends, finding companionship, or of a dating relationship have filled the need formerly filled by a poor substitute. He no longer masturbates because he doesn't need to. He has grown up, matured, and "put away childish things."

My wife and I brought up our three children on the basis of this attitude toward masturbation. When there is openness of communication on the subject of sex, including masturbation, we can testify that it will be simply an incidental part of growing up and not become a major problem. As one of my teenagers said to me one day when we were talking about it, "Don't worry, dad; it's sure no big deal with me!" I think that sums up my view. It's high time we stop making such a "big deal" out of masturbation and give it the well-deserved unimportance it merits.

Courtship and premarital sex. The American system of dating and courtship leading up to engagement and marriage creates certain sex problems which are not found in many parts of the world. Where the choice of a mate is largely the decision of parents and done at certain particular periods in the life of the youth, many of our sex problems are by-passed. Perhaps this is why there is almost no direct teaching in Scripture related to this subject. The whole sociological system then was entirely different and would be impossible to use in giving us guidelines on courtship and premarital sex. In those days, as would be the case today in many Eastern lands, any kind of physical or erotic contact between a man and a woman—even a touch on the hand— would be considered an invitation to intercourse.

It is futile to look for specific regulations from Scripture which might apply to our system of dating and courtship with its varying degrees of physical intimacy. Thus it is very difficult to answer the favorite sixty-four-dollar question of youth today: How far can a Christian go? Again we must depend upon scriptural principles as they relate to certain physical and psychological facts concerning the nature of sex.

Ideally there should be a balanced progression between friendship, love, and sex; they should develop at the same pace. However, they seldom do, and in this sex-saturated society of ours there is almost a built-in guarantee of an overemphasis upon the physical. This is particularly true of what Frank Cox calls the "sexual stress period."[17] This is the time prior to marriage when sexual desires are at a peak, when the entire mass media and advertising world uses every possible means to stimulate those desires, and when the automobile offers almost unlimited freedom from external restraints. To make the problem all the more acute, a large segment of Christianity has joined with secular thinkers in throwing overboard the authority of all former moral landmarks and in promoting a carefully thought-out version of "New Morality."[18] Some of these, supposedly written from a Christian standpoint, go to remarkable extremes including in their approval premarital intercourse and even some instances of adultery, wife-swapping, and practical bigamy.[19] For evangelical Christians there is little help from those offering "A Revolutionary New Sex Guide for the Now Generation of Christians."[20]

Let us look at the nature of sexual excitement and see if this can furnish us with the basis of some guidelines for Christian standards. God has made sex so that it is progressive and leads ultimately to intercourse and its climax in orgasm. This includes a built-in "law of diminishing returns" which demands more and more, with an increasing crescendo of arousal and excitement until there is a place where the will no longer effectively functions and the emotions take over completely. Our youth need to be taught this very carefully so when they experience this progression they will understand themselves as "normal" and not necessarily "sinful." They should realize this is actually a part of what is technically the "foreplay" meant to lead up to sexual intercourse and is, therefore, to be treated seriously and sacredly.

From a Christian standpoint it is impossible to separate the sexual from the personal since sex is personal communication and commitment. There are degrees of personal commitment and degrees of physical involvement. Some of the physical are casual with little or no involvement, as say, holding hands. Others as they become more intimate, mean deeper involvement and commitment, for example, close bodily contact or a sustained kiss. Thus as there is a progression of excitement, there is also a progression of involvement, commitment, and responsibility. It is impossible, from a Christian standpoint, to separate the two, for sexual expression symbolizes the intensity and depth of the relationship. Sexual integrity and personal integrity are inseparable.

In light of these facts many casual physical intimacies that take place in the typical American courtship scene should have no place among Christians. Sustained kissing, or long times of necking in parked cars are not activities that can be carelessly thrown around, for they are symbols intended to carry more meaning for the Christian. To simply use one another as biological and sexual playthings is to live "as the Gentiles do," and to "surrender to sensuality" which Paul admonishes against in Ephesians 4:17–21 (Phillips).

But what about Christians who are seriously "in love" with each other and have committed themselves to marriage? People in love want to express that love to each other, and this certainly will include physical expression. What are the limits of that expression outside of marriage? The Scripture forbids such a couple to have sexual intercourse. Some ten references in Scripture list "fornication" as an evil;[21] and about an equal number of times it is expressly forbidden.[22] *Fornication* is intercourse between the unmarried; *adultery* involves someone married.

In Scripture God gives a clear absolute governing full sexual union: it is limited to the marriage relationship. It is a law, but it is a law of love. Jesus describes love as a new commandment (John 13:34; 15:12). Anyone who has counseled recognizes the utter naïveté of the idea that love dispenses with the necessity of laws because it has a built-in regulating device, a sort of moral compass, which will always guide us like a homing pigeon to right moral behavior. The ultimate question of love is, How shall I behave? When Paul answers this in his great love chapter (1 Cor. 13), he gives us some definite guidelines, the majority of which are *negative*. The moral commandments of God, both positive and negative, give the content of love; they tell us what is expected of love. Certainly they are secondary to love, but they cannot be contrary to it. "If you love me, you will keep my commandments," said Jesus (John 14:15, RSV); in doing so he was not asking us to do anything which he himself didn't do. "If you keep my commandments, you will abide in my love, just as I have kept my Father's commandments and abide in his love" (John 15:10, RSV).

The scriptural reasons for limiting intercourse to marriage are not negative but positive, namely, the nature of man and the nature of sex. In intercourse two persons become "one flesh"; they are then considered indivisible. Both the Old Testament analogy of the covenant relation between God and Israel and the New Testament analogy of the relationship between Christ and his church confirm this. Scripture never even hints that premarital intercourse is wrong for the many pragmatic reasons we offer (or should I say threaten) our youth—like the possibility of pregnancy, venereal disease, or better chances of a happy marriage. It is the positive reason based on what man is and what his relationship to God and to others must be. The modern question, not is it wrong, but is it meaningful? is in itself wrong. How can it be meaningful when it violates the stated limitations and meaning God intended it to have? To override the Creator's word can only bring about the wrong meaning.

But what about many sexual activities between steady or

engaged couples which stop short of actual intercourse? How often I have heard a couple tell me they "have done everything but . . ." This means that they are petting to the stage of achieving orgasm. Harvey Cox calls this "technical virginity." In a discussion I once had with some Christian college students they termed it "the evangelical substitute for adultery."

Although there is no direct scriptural word on this kind of petting or "making out," when put into the context of the progressive nature of sexual activity and God's intended purpose for intercourse, it would seem to come under the general condemnation of lust and the loss of control over one's bodily appetites. At best it is a very dangerous game to play, and many Christians who start it find they then are driven to go "all the way." In any case, they are plagued with deep guilt, lose respect for themselves and their partners, and often find themselves picking at each other and quarreling so that they end up destroying the very love they were intending to express.

An article in *Seventeen* magazine (July, 1965) written by two psychologists and entitled "Sex and the Teen-Age Girl" confirms this.

> Some studies show that twice as many engagements are broken among couples who have had intercourse. . . . Furthermore . . . [these couples] are more likely to be divorced or separated or to indulge in adultery. One way or another, premarital intimacy is more closely connected to broken relationships than to solid ties.

Honest and open communication between the couple and a prayerful commitment to setting agreed limits to their lovemaking will go a long way toward helping them maintain their controls and their personal integrity. It is not easy, but it certainly brings great rewards when the intimacies of petting and foreplay are kept for the marriage bed.

SEX WITHIN MARRIAGE

If the preceding section dealt with some important nega-
tives, it did so only in order to make this section all the more
positive. Full sexual expression in the one-flesh union of
intercourse is restricted to marriage, not to limit its enjoyment, but to enhance it. Jesus' words immediately following
those about keeping his commandments because of love are
especially applicable to the ecstasies of sex within marriage:
"That your joy may be full!" (John 15:11, RSV). There is
increasing evidence from every angle—spiritual, psychological, and sociological—that God's design for sex and marriage is sure proof that he delights in giving his children
"every good thing."

Marriage is the final expression of love and personal
commitment; it is a covenant between lovers to spend their
lives together. Sexual intercourse is likewise the final physical and emotional expression of that love and commitment.
How wonderful that in God's plan they literally come together at the same time. Dwight Hervey Small writes:

> The one-flesh union is so profound, so intimate, so enduring
> that only marriage can encompass it. Scripturally, monogamy
> is demanded, not by specific texts, but by the recognition that
> this one-flesh union is the total union of marriage; a total re-
> lationship can exist only in the form of monogamy.[23]

The genius of Small's book is caught in its very title, *Christian, Celebrate Your Sexuality.* To Christians, sex is indeed
a celebration. That celebration began with the Creator himself, for although five times before God had said of some
new aspect of his creation, "It is good," it was not until he
created male and female that he declared exultantly, "It is
very good!" For too long many Christians have been affected by false guilts and sub-Christian ideas about sex.
Thank God, we have finally caught up with the Scriptures,

which, though they warn against all kinds of sexual sins, also describe the beauty and joy of sex. In Genesis 26:6, Isaac is said to be "fondling" his wife Rebecca. Even the reserved, modest King James Version says he is "sporting" with his wife—certainly a rather free description of marital lovemaking. And if the Song of Solomon was published in a really modern translation, it might even be banned in Boston. Clearly Scripture not only allows sexual intercourse; it endorses and encourages it. "Do not cheat each other of normal sexual intercourse, unless of course you both decide to abstain temporarily for fasting . . . but afterward you should resume relations as before" (1 Cor. 7:3, Phillips). What a basic misunderstanding among some Christians that they are too "spiritual" to enjoy sex to the full! In light of the creation story and the whole biblical philosophy of sex, this idea is not only heresy, it is almost blasphemy. It is calling unclean what God has called clean and calling bad what God has called "very good."

One practical question is often asked me by conscientious Christian married couples: What is right or wrong? Is it okay to do this or that? One simple Christian principle governs the answer to all such questions: Anything that is physically enjoyable, emotionally fulfilling, and mutually agreeable is morally right. The important phrase here is "mutually agreeable" since at the heart of married love is respect for the partner's wishes and a desire to please. Outside of this governing principle there are no taboos, no restrictions, except that of loving and caring about the other person. Certainly the only law in lovemaking is the law of love.

I sense a growing trend in this whole area of sex inside and outside marriage. There seems to be a movement toward what is basically the Christian philosophy because we are learning the hard way that anything else goes against the created order of things and ultimately does not work out. The following headlines and articles are arranged in chronological order:

Time magazine, August 21, 1972. Cover story, "Sex and the Teen-ager."

Newsweek magazine, November 27, 1972. Cover story, "The New Sex Therapy."

Newsweek magazine, July 16, 1973. Cover story, "Games Singles Play."

Time magazine, October 1, 1973. Whoopee! *Playboy* announces the results of its great sex poll! All statistics are up! Freedom has come at last! Americans are finally liberated from their Puritan and Christian heritage. But wait. Not so fast. What's happening now?

Time magazine, November 25, 1974. Avant-Garde Retreat . . . Swinging sex is definitely on the decline. Many sex clubs are disappearing. In 1973 there were twenty such clubs in southern California; now there are only eight. Tom Palmer, former executive director of the Sexual Freedom League, has now turned toward midget auto racing! The sociologists and predictors are taking a second look. Why? "There is now a strong desire for connectedness."

Redbook magazine, February 1975, in an issue on "The Marriage Boom, a Nationwide Report, Who Gets Married Today—and Why" states some of these startling conclusions (pp. 85–90):

> The need to be married—the ageless yearning of one man and one woman to pledge themselves to each other for life in a lawful relationship, is reasserting itself everywhere in the U.S.A. . . . Thousands of couples, of all ages, races, and religions . . . who a few years ago scorned the idea of marriage are marrying today legally and with ritual; and though it is expressed in myriad ways they are all marrying for a single reason: commitment. Commitment is the key to it all. . . . The reassessment of marriage is also bringing deeper fulfillment . . . . people are now interested in having more meaningful relationships.

Commitment, relationships, pledges, one man, one woman. How utterly square! How unbelievably old-fashioned! How delightfully Christian! How good to know we were right all along. And of course, there's a reason for it all. Our sexuality is rooted in creation; it is a part of God's divine order and, as in other areas, "When in doubt refer to the manufacturer's handbook."

Human love, with its fullest expression in sexual union, is a spark—a gift from God's burning heart of love. That spark can lift us to the highest heights of ecstasy, joy, and wonder.

And if that's just a spark, what must be the flame?

NOTES

1. Dwight Hervey Small, *Christian Celebrate Your Sexuality.* (New Jersey: Fleming H. Revell, 1974). See part 2, pp. 104–205 for a scholarly development of this idea.

2. Karl Menninger, *Whatever Became of Sin?* (New York: Hawthorn, 1973), p. 36.

3. Ronald L. Koteskey, head of the Psychology Department, Asbury College, in an unpublished paper entitled "Masturbation" (1975), notes the strange silence on this subject by both secular and Christian authors. He states he was able to find only three books written on the subject (in English) in the past 35 years. *Psychological Abstracts,* while indexing almost every other sexual topic, does not even mention masturbation until 1973. Two articles on the subject have appeared in *Pastoral Psychology.* The first, written in 1954, promised another article "in an early issue," but the article does not appear until 6 years—57 issues—later. *Pastoral Counselor* does not have a single article on it and neither does *The Journal of Pastoral Care* in its entire 27-year history.

4. W. Stekel, *Auto-eroticism,* trans. J. S. Van Teslaar (New York: Liveright, 1950). Stekel takes the position that every sexual act done without the cooperation of another person, in-

cluding fantasies and unconscious desires, is a form of masturbation.

5. William Hulme, *Youth Considers Sex* (New York: Thomas Nelson and Sons, 1965), p. 41.

6. Sex Information and Educational Council of the United States (SIECUS), *Sexuality and Man* (New York: Scribner's, 1970), p. 63.

7. Jack Wyrtzen, *Youth's Purity Problems* (Chicago: Moody, 1954), p. 25.

8. Menninger, *Whatever Became of Sin?* p. 35.

9. J. E. Adams, *The Christian Counselor's Manual* (Grand Rapids: Baker Book House, 1973), pp. 399–402.

10. T. J. Bingham, "Pastoral and ethical notes on problems of masturbation," *Pastoral Psychology* 11 (1960): 19–23.

11. H. J. Miles, *Sexual Understanding before Marriage* (Grand Rapids: Zondervan, 1971), pp. 137–62.

12. M. O. Vincent, *God, Sex, and You* (Philadelphia: Lippincott, 1971), pp. 142–44.

13. Hulme, *Youth Considers Sex,* pp. 40–51.

14. Charlie W. Shedd, *The Stork Is Dead* (Waco, Tex.: Word Books, 1968), pp. 64–73.

15. Menninger, *Whatever Became of Sin?* p. 31.

16. SIECUS, *Sexuality and Man,* p. 69.

17. Frank D. Cox, *Youth, Marriage, and the Seductive Society* (Dubuque, Iowa: Wm. C. Brown, 1967), p. 21.

18. The following is a partial list of the more well-known books which take such a position: Joseph Fletcher, *Situation Ethics;* Rustum and Della Roy, *Honest Sex;* John A. T. Robinson, *Christian Morals Today* and *Honest to God;* Frederick C. Wood, *Sex and The New Morality;* Alastair Heron, ed., *Towards a Quaker View of Sex;* Norman Pittenger, *Making Sexuality Human;* Richard F. Hettlinger, *Living With Sex.*

19. Rustum and Della Roy, *Honest Sex* (a revolutionary new sex guide for the now generation of Christians) (New York: New American Library. Signet Books, 1969), pp. 67 ff., 75, 93–94, 100.

20. Ibid.

21. Matt. 15:19; Mark 7:21; Acts 15:20, 29; 21:15; Rom. 1:29; 1 Cor. 5:1; 2 Cor. 12:21; Gal. 5:19; Eph. 5:3; Col. 3:5.

22. 1 Cor. 6:13, 18; Eph. 5:3; 1 Thess. 4:3; 1 Cor. 6:18; 10:8.

23. Small, *Celebrate Your Sexuality,* p. 178.

Study Guide

The purpose of a study guide is to help individuals or groups of readers to better understand, evaluate and interact with the ideas that are presented in a book or collection of articles. The chapters which comprise the preceding pages contain a number of insights and sometimes conflicting opinions, written by capable people who have given serious thought to the various aspects of human sexuality. By adding a study guide, it is hoped that you will be encouraged and helped to think back over what has been written and to arrive at some further conclusions of your own.

It is possible, of course, to work through this study guide alone, but probably you would find group discussion to be more beneficial and interesting. The following study guide, therefore, has been designed for group reaction and interaction. Whenever a group meets, there should be a leader who can guide the discussion and stimulate interaction. The same leader could direct all of the discussions, but you may want to shift leadership responsibilities so that a different person, chosen from the group, leads each of the sessions.

Before meeting, each group member should read the chapter or chapters to be discussed and look over the questions which follow. These questions are designed to stimulate discussion and at times may lead to lively debate. The leader should encourage everyone to express his or her views, should maintain a somewhat objective perspective in the group, and should try to keep the discussion from getting too far off the track. When there are irreconcilable differences, the leader should have the right to stop discussion until more homework can be done, expert advice can be obtained, or the group agrees that discussion has reached a dead end.

One final comment: the questions and exercises which follow are merely suggestive. If you can think of questions which are better, use them. If the discussion brings up issues which are important but not in the study guide or chapter, consider them. Your experience as a group might be more fun that way, and hopefully this will be a worthwhile learning experience.

Chapter 1: Women and Men: How Different Should We Be?
Letha Scanzoni

In this first chapter, Letha Scanzoni gets to the heart of the problem of sexual identity. Writing clearly and incisively the author criticizes the widely held view that "regardless of individual abilities, interests and proclivities, persons have been expected to fill a role according to their sex. . . . males are expected to behave one way and females another." As you read this chapter, ask yourself the following questions: Is it really necessary for males to behave differently than females? Apart from physiological differences, are men really different from women? What would happen to me if instead of trying to fit someone else's definition of masculinity or femininity, I tried to develop my unique personal abilities, interests, and inclinations?

MEETING TOGETHER

1. As you come together for your first group discussion, arrange your chairs in a circle, if this is possible. Each member of

the group should give his or her name, and then for a few minutes group members should (a) share why they are in the group and (b) indicate what they hope to accomplish in the group. Perhaps you can agree on a list of goals for the group discussions. Decide, too, whether there will be one leader or a sharing of leadership responsibilities between several group members. How frequently will you meet? For how long each time? These preliminary discussions will help you to know each other better and get your group off to a good start.

2. Scanzoni writes about male and female *activities* (the things we are supposed to do because of our sex) and about male and female *attributes* (the characteristics we are supposed to possess because of our sex). In our society, what are the activities and attributes that are supposed to characterize a "truly masculine male"? Make a similar list of the activities and attributes for the "truly feminine female."

3. In view of the above lists, how do you respond to the statement that "sexes have far more in common than they have differences. Thus, today . . . ascribed roles on the basis of gender seem totally out of place. *Individual* capabilities and achievements and personalities are what count, not one's membership in a certain category labeled . . . 'male' or 'female.' . . . It puzzles me that so many Christians find this threatening and, in some cases, are calling for a more extreme and rigid segregation of sex roles than ever before."

4. As Christians it is important for us to determine whether or not there are divinely assigned roles for males and females. Read Galatians 3:28 and then turn to 1 Peter 3:1–7. Is it possible for women to be equal with men *and* submissive? Is this the relationship that Christ had with the Father (Phil. 2:5–11)?

5. Do you agree with Scanzoni that the whole idea of labeling characteristics "masculine" or "feminine" is unscriptural? Give reasons and biblical support for your answers.

6. "Many Christians fear that doing away with clearly defined sex roles in terms of gender-assigned activities and attributes will confuse children about their sexual identity." Do you agree?

Suppose we were able to eliminate sex roles. Would this be bad for the society or for you? Would it be unbiblical?

CONCLUDING COMMENTS

The role of women and of men is a vitally important and hotly debated issue outside of the church and within. Church leaders must help people to clarify their thinking on this issue, but such clarification begins with a careful and open-minded study of all the scriptural references to men and women. As believers we must resist the all-too-prevalent tendency to come to the Bible with preconceived notions about sex roles and attempts to make the Scriptures support our opinions. Letha Scanzoni has raised a significant question in this chapter: men and women—how different should we be?

Chapter 2: Changes in Marital Gender Roles—
Authority to Affirmation
John Scanzoni

In his chapter, John Scanzoni writes about the importance of men and women affirming each other, especially in marriage. As you read the chapter, ask yourself, "How can I affirm other people, especially my spouse?" What difference will this make in you? Before meeting with your group, read the biblical accounts of the life of Priscilla and her husband Aquila (Acts 18:1–3, 24–6; Rom. 16:3–5).

MEETING TOGETHER

1. What does John Scanzoni mean by "individual affirmation"? How did Aquila affirm Priscilla? Does this biblical marriage really have any relevance for us today?
2. According to the chapter, "Aquila's behavior is our model" in that Aquila did four things for his wife. What are these four

things? Should a modern husband do these things for his wife? Should the wife also do these things for her husband? Is this husband-wife example a good model for every Christian marriage? What about your marriage?

3. In his chapter, Scanzoni describes the female producer of Sesame Street whose husband works without salary in volunteer work. Do you know couples who have reversed roles like this (the wife works while the husband stays home or does volunteer work)? Is this unbiblical? Is it an acceptable life-style if both husband and wife agree? Would it work for you? Why not?

4. Scanzoni believes that after a few years husbands and wives often grow tired of each other because the husband is growing in his career while the wife at home has nothing to contribute that is fresh and exciting. Is this an accurate picture of marriages today? What about your marriage? How can this trend towards marital boredom be stopped?

5. In his chapter, the author criticizes the view that there must be "greater recognition of male headship and authority." He especially is critical of popular movements which advise wives to "use sex to manipulate their husbands in subtle or covert fashion," or which picture the father as a hammer, the wife as a chisel and the child as stone in a "chain of command." What do you think of these viewpoints? Are they biblical? Can there be both "individual affirmation" between the sexes and "greater recognition of man headship and authority"?

CONCLUDING COMMENTS

John Scanzoni has pointed to an important issue in this chapter: the view that both men and women should be free to develop their God-given talents, abilities, and gifts. A persisting and unresolved problem concerns whether male authority is or should be more important than the development of these individual abilities in the husband and wife. Because the church is failing to provide answers to these questions, hundreds of people are turning to books or popular seminars. What can your church do to help men and women both develop freely as God meant them to be, and fulfill the scripturally based roles for males and females?

Chapter 3: Femininity Today:
Walking the Knife-Edge
Mary Stewart Van Leeuwen

Mary Stewart Van Leeuwen is concise and to the point in this excellent answer to some of the questions that have been raised in the preceeding chapters. Do you think "walking the knife-edge" is a good subtitle for a paper on femininity today? Has the author really given practical suggestions for the woman who is walking the knife-edge and is struggling with what it means to be feminine? With what do you agree in this paper? With what do you disagree? How do the author's conclusions effect your life? What is the relevance of the chapter for men?

MEETING TOGETHER

1. Van Leeuwen identifies two "fundamentally incompatible positions regarding femininity, or womanhood, each insisting that the weight of Scripture, history, science, and common sense is on its side." What are these two positions? Do you agree that "there is some solid basis for *each* of these views in Scripture" or that "one has merely to select judiciously and argue cleverly in order to make an almost watertight case for either point of view"?

2. Have someone in your group read Proverbs 31:10–31. Could this be used by either of the feminine positions? How does Van Leeuwen deal with the controversy between the two positions? Do you agree? Why?

3. Van Leeuwen concludes that the dilemma over sex roles will never be resolved theologically. According to her chapter why does she make this assertion? Do you agree that the Holy Spirit calls each of us to steep ourselves "in the Word as a whole, in an attitude of openness and obedience, and then to be prepared for some surprises," even in terms of the unique sex roles that might develop?

4. The author severely criticizes those who decide what every female (or male) should be like and then decide that "if all my friends don't do the same, they are brainwashed, narrow, and irresponsible Christians." Do you think this really happens? Are *you* guilty of adhering to a model of femininity (or masculinity) and criticizing those who don't fit?

5. This chapter makes the interesting suggestion that strong advocates of any one women's role may be reacting to their past. "I cannot stress strongly enough the necessity to grow beyond this attitude," Van Leeuwen writes, "especially if there is in it any trace of bitterness or a vindictive satisfaction in 'getting back' at the people who have wronged you and limited you in times past." Do you agree that strong positions on femininity may reflect a reaction against the past? Is this true of you? What can be done about this?

6. The chapter concludes with a suggestion that decisions about one's sex roles must be made both on the basis of what brings personal sanctification, and what builds up God's Kingdom. Do you think it is true that if we are concerned about our responsibilities as Christians in the world, our roles as women and men "will take care of themselves?"

CONCLUDING COMMENTS

Is it possible that we have given so much attention to the problem of defining male and female roles, that we have forgotten to be sensitive to the Spirit's guiding for each of our lives? The Bible laid down some broad principles of femininity and masculinity, but never is there a rigid blueprint for all to follow in building their lives as women and men. Can we, in the church, therefore tolerate individual differences in gifts and life-styles, so long as these differences do not violate the clear teaching of the Bible? Perhaps this is one way in which we can achieve "role liberation for the Christian."

Chapter 4: Masculinity Today
Gary R. Collins

The first three chapters in this book put most emphasis on the sexual roles of women. But it is important to remember that as women's roles change this will also influence men. Already, masculine roles are changing whether men like it or not. In this chapter, Gary Collins looks at the traditional image of masculinity, shows how this is changing, and suggests an alternative view of what it means to be masculine. As you read, especially the last section of the chapter, ask yourself if Collins's portrait of masculinity is really feasible, complete and/or consistent with the Bible. What does it have to say about you as a man (or about your husband if you are female)? Before meeting in your group read Ephesians 5:1–6:20. Does this whole passage have relevance for masculinity?

MEETING TOGETHER

1. In his chapter, Collins summarizes and criticizes what he calls "the masculine image." Is the author's summary of traditional masculinity accurate? What do you think of the three stated problems with this stereotyped masculine image (it's harmful, unrealistic, and crumbling)?

2. The author claims that for men, especially, self-esteem and feelings of security are closely tied to the belief that "I am masculine." If this is true, does it follow that men will be threatened as traditional views of masculinity crumble? How can we help men handle these changes in popular views of masculinity?

3. This chapter suggests that many men react to the "masculine dilemma" in one of several ways. Do you know of men who react in one or more of these ways? What about you or your husband? Are there better ways to respond to the masculine dilemma?

4. Collins lists five marks of the truly masculine male. Do you agree with this description of masculine identity? What would you add or subtract from the list? Why? If you are a man, how do you plan to change as a result of having read this chapter?

5. Someone has suggested that while Collins maintains that "a clearly defined male and female sexual identity is critically important," his five marks of masculinity could apply equally well to femininity. Is this a valid criticism? Does leadership within the home set men apart as being uniquely masculine? How then can a man be masculine if he is unmarried or living alone? How can you be more masculine?

CONCLUDING COMMENTS

With so much emphasis on women's roles during the past few years, the meaning of masculinity has been neglected, especially within the church. Men, especially insecure men, are often threatened by religion, lest it appear that they are weak and have to rely on a theological crutch. Surely now, more than ever before, the church must help men to see what it means to be masculine, especially in the home. What is your church doing to help men? What could it be doing?

Chapter 5: A Christian Model
for Sexual Understanding and Behavior
Harry N. Hollis, Jr.

Sex, of course, involves more than roles or characteristics which we label masculine or feminine. Sex involves physical arousal, intense pleasure, and intimacy between people. It involves guilt, frustration, fantasy and struggles with self-discipline —and too often it involves exploitation of others along with self-centered hedonism. Harry Hollis directs our attention to all of these attitudes in his chapter on sexual understanding and behavior. As you read, try to apply the chapter to yourself. Ask "What is *my* attitude towards sex?" "Do I misuse or abuse God's gift of sex?" "Am I too self-centered, lacking in self-discipline, or unappreciative of sex?" "How can *my* sexuality be more satisfying and consistent with God's plan for sex?"

MEETING TOGETHER

1. According to Hollis there are four purposes of sexual intercourse. Read each of the following Scripture verses which the author lists in his chapter: Genesis 2:24 (union), Genesis 1:28 (procreation), Proverbs 5:18–19 (pleasure), Genesis 4:1 (communication). Can you think of other Bible verses dealing with sexual intercourse?

2. Do you think it really appropriate to thank God for sex? Some people have maintained that sex and religion don't mix. What do you think? Read 1 Corinthians 6:15–7:5. Does it seem strange that the Scriptures should mix discussions about sexual intercourse with commands to glorify God with our bodies?

3. How do you respond to the following quotations from Hollis's chapter?

> We do not have sex; we are sexual beings. To talk about sex only in physical terms is to miss what the Bible teaches. The body and soul are knit together in such a way that one is affected by the other. This unity of personhood stands against casual intercourse because the attempt to limit intercourse to physical involvement and pleasure is contrary to the biblical teachings about the nature of human beings.

> Praise to the Creator can involve the guiltless appreciation and intense enjoyment of the pleasure of intercourse. . . . Praising the Creator for sex can also keep us from taking sex too lightly or too seriously. When we see that God has made us sexual beings, we will neither belittle sex nor make it a god. . . . We can show appreciation for creation by treating others as persons and not things.

> In seeking to restrain the misuses of sex, moralism will be of little help. Instead, we must deal with the anxiety and emotional impoverishment which have led to sexual misbehavior. . . . The spiritual transformation of the individual must be

accompanied by an understanding of the psychological dynamics of sex.

4. Hollis states that sex should be controlled and used for God's purposes. How can this be done? How can we restrain sexual evil in our own lives and in our society, as Hollis suggests? Try to give practical answers.

5. This chapter assumes that God has acted and is acting in the world as Creator, Judge and Redeemer. Summarize how Hollis ties in his discussion of sex with these three actions of God. What is your opinion of this "model"?

CONCLUDING COMMENTS

The Bible says a great deal about sex, but we rarely consider this subject in the church. How can your church help people to thank God for sex, to learn sexual self-discipline, and to understand the biblical teachings about sex? According to Hollis, "Without adopting the world's standards, the church must openly listen and minister to people with varied sexual life-styles. The church can influence society as a whole by holding up the ideal of sexual intercourse within a loving marriage covenant. It can help homosexuals find the aid they need to be the sexual beings God intended. It can work to make certain that the laws not only protect society from sexual offenders but also provide programs for the rehabilitation of these offenders. The church can work for responsible programs of sex education. It can reject discrimination against women and work for human liberation through Christ." Are these practical suggestions for a Christian approach to sexual understanding and behavior?

Chapter 6: Christian Sex Counseling
Ed Wheat

In his chapter, Ed Wheat takes us to the heart of sexuality and discusses the act of sexual intercourse from the perspective of a family physician. As you read the chapter ask how it applies to your own sexual behavior. Are there facts in Wheat's presentation which can help you to have more satisfying sexual experiences in your marriage? If you are single, does this chapter have any relevance for you?

MEETING TOGETHER

1. Wheat indicates that the material of this chapter is "intimate information" which usually is presented only to couples in marital or premarital counseling sessions. Do you think there is value in discussing this chapter in your group? Are there reasons for not discussing it?

2. The chapter makes reference to several passages of Scripture. Have someone read the following verses to the group: Mark 10:6–9; 1 Corinthians 7:3–5; 1 Timothy 4:1–4; Hebrews 13:4. What, if anything, do these verses say to Christians about sex?

3. What is your reaction to the following quotations from Wheat's chapter. Do you agree? Why?

> The only activity which is to interrupt briefly the normal sex relations between a Christian man and his wife is fasting and prayer. Today this means that one or the other of the marriage partners feels a burden to ask God in prayer to accomplish a specific spiritual ministry in the life of another person.

> The art of love is largely a savoring of each phase of the experience, seeking maximum perception of sensation, rather than working and hurrying toward release. Achieving orgasm is the very thing that ends the sexual enjoyment. Every physical union should be a contest to see which partner can outplease the other.

> Many sexual frustrations could be solved if husbands and wives talked a little bit more.

> . . . sex pleasures or problems should never be discussed with friends or family, and no one should joke about any of these private matters.

> There is really a far greater dimension to the sexual relationship for the mature Christian couple who have a total commit-

ment to Jesus Christ. . . . When this type of relationship exists, the sexual union becomes even an act of worship.

4. What is your reaction to Wheat's comments about Jesus Christ near the end of his paper? Does this have any personal relevance for you? Does it have relevance to the issue of human sexuality?

5. Wheat maintains that "the wife views the sex act as a part of the total relationship with her husband. This means that every meaningful, fully enjoyable sex act really begins with a loving, attentive attitude which may begin hours or even days before. This requires both partners to assume the responsibility for giving their total self—physically, emotionally, and spiritually— so that the sex act becomes a dynamic technique to express fully unselfish love one for the other." What does this say about pre-marital or extramarital sex? Can you give a convincing argument why sexual intercourse should be restricted to a married couple within marriage?

CONCLUDING COMMENTS

What is your church doing to help married couples develop a better sexual relationship? Should the church give counseling similar to that suggested by Wheat in his paper? If so, is your church doing this? If not, why not—and who should give the counseling instead? Does the Christian bring anything unique to sexual counseling which would not be mentioned by the non-Christian counselor?

Chapter 7
A Biblical View of Homosexuality
Dennis F. Kinlaw

This chapter and the one which follows direct our attention to sexuality between persons of the same sex. With the rise of the

Gay Liberation movement, this issue of homosexuality has attracted considerable attention both outside of the church and
within. Before discussing these next two chapters, it could be
helpful for you to look up the major Bible verses dealing with
homosexuality: Genesis 19:1–28; Leviticus 18:22, 26–29; 20:13;
Romans 1:18–32; 1 Corinthians 6:9, 10.

MEETING TOGETHER

1. Dennis Kinlaw begins his chapter with a basic but extremely important discussion of the authority of the Bible. Ask
someone in the group to read aloud the second and third
paragraphs of Kinlaw's chapter. Do you agree with this view?
If not, on what basis can you reach a conclusion about homosexuality? If so, how do you react to the fourth paragraph of
Kinlaw's chapter?

2. Kinlaw maintains that sex outside of marriage (including
homosexuality) is viewed within the Bible as a form of idolatry.
What is your reaction to this suggestion?

3. Read the following exerpts from Kinlaw's chapter:

"The thrust of the Scriptures is clear. Sexual activity is intended for a male and a female within the bonds of marriage.
All sexual intercourse between persons outside this bond,
whether between persons of the same sex or of the opposite,
is an abomination in the sight of God and evokes his wrath.
Anything that ignores this is game playing. . . . Homosexuality is thus a perversion. . . ."

Do you agree with this quotation? (Look again at 1 Cor. 6:9–10.)
Is it possible to accept Kinlaw's conclusion but still show compassion for homosexuals? Suppose you eliminate the word *intercourse* from the above quotation and substitute the word *attraction*. Would you still feel the same about the quotation?
What if we substitute *lust* in place of *intercourse*?

4. Assume that a member of your discussion group confesses,
"I am a Christian but I am strongly attracted to members of my
own sex." How would you respond to this person? Would you
agree with Kinlaw that (a) you are "dealing with a matter of
gravest significance" and (b) "God's grace is available to . . .

(the homosexual group member) as to all the rest of this lost and blighted race"?

5. In this chapter, the author summarizes several of the arguments that are used by some Christians to "explain away" the Bible verses dealing with homosexuality. What are these arguments? What is your opinion of them?

CONCLUDING COMMENTS

We are living in an age when homosexuality is being more and more openly accepted as a viable life-style even for Christians. It is important, therefore, that believers know where they stand on this issue. Do you agree that overt homosexuality is sinful? What about homosexual tendencies? Can homosexuality be changed? What is your attitude to the marriage of homosexuals, the ordination of homosexuals and the adoption of children by homosexuals? How would you counsel a homosexual who wants to change? How would you counsel with a homosexual who has no desire to change?

Chapter 8
The Church and the Homosexual
Guy Charles

Guy Charles openly admits that prior to his conversion he was a practicing homosexual for more than thirty-seven years. Because of this, Charles has a special understanding of the homosexual's life-style and way of thinking. What is your attitude towards homosexuality? Are you critical? sympathetic? accepting? repulsed? threatened? Do you have any homosexual impulses yourself? How are they influencing you? What are you doing about them?

MEETING TOGETHER

1. Charles criticizes those persons within the church who refuse to have fellowship with homosexuals and deny them "the

ability to approach God, once the homosexual's personal life-style has been made common knowledge." Is this a problem in your church? Are *you* guilty of rejecting homosexuals as people and refusing to show compassion towards them?

2. Is it possible, in our desire to show compassion, that we overlook the Bible's statements about homosexual behavior and silently give our approval to a homosexual life-style? Should we accept within our congregations "those who have affirmed homosexual life-styles and are seeking companionship which allows them to retain both the life-style and their religion"?

3. Charles states that many homosexuals live with fear—especially the fear of being discovered. Perhaps there are people in your church or in your group who have such fears. How can we help such persons? Is it possible for secret homosexuals to get help from the church even if they keep their secret to themselves? Might it be better if the homosexual met with a counselor? Read James 5:16 and 1 John 1:9.

4. Do you think there is a difference between overt homosexual acts and a secret homosexuality which has never led to overt acts? Is one of these worse than the other? What about Charles's statement that "homosexuality is not contained in the sexual act alone. It can be a lust within the eye, the touch or the mind"? Do you agree that homosexuality is "a choice of the will"? Read Matthew 5:28–30 out loud, then turn to Romans 12:1–2. Do these scriptures have anything to say about sexually unhealthy thoughts, fantasies or inclinations?

5. What is your reaction to Charles's eight-point suggestion for helping homosexuals? Will this work? Could it help a homosexual who does not want to change? Could it help you in any way?

CONCLUDING COMMENTS

Homosexuality is just one example of sex outside of marriage. What are some other examples? What should our attitude be towards these forms of sexuality? Does the sexual looseness which pervades our culture contribute to deviant sex? If so, what can we do as Christians to offset or reverse these influences in the society, in the home, in youth, in the church? Are you really dealing with these issues in your church? These are questions which demand answers from sensitive and thoughtful Christian leaders.

Chapter 9
Sex Education in the Home
Letha Scanzoni

In this sensitive and practical chapter, Letha Scanzoni deals with the specifics of educating children about sexuality. The author's view of sex education is consistent with the general instructions about religious teaching found in Deuteronomy 6:1–7 and Proverbs 6:20–22. Read these passages and also 1 Thessalonians 4:1–5. What is the relevance of these verses for sex education?

MEETING TOGETHER

1. Scanzoni is critical of parents (even well-intentioned parents) who try to shield their children from sexual knowledge. Do you agree that parents who withhold sexual information are really failing their children and handing them over to other sources of information—like magazines or young friends who may also be poorly informed?

2. What is your reaction to the following quotations: "A book for physicians suggests that they see some of the erotic films and read some of the sexually explicit books available today in order to become better counselors by understanding the milieu in which young persons are growing up. I think that's wise advice for parents, pastors, and other counselors too." Is Philippians 4:8 relevant in this discussion? Without exposure to such erotic material is it possible for parents and others to become out of touch with what their children are experiencing?

3. Scanzoni describes the plight of a Christian teenager who wrote: "I worry many times about what the Lord thinks of just

how far you should go with your boyfriend or girlfriend. Just how far is too far? And if it *is* too far, how do you say no?" How would you answer this teenager? Is this a part of sex education?

4. What is the difference between a sex ethic based on hedonism and one based on humanism? If a "significant number of Christian young people" are taking the humanism view seriously, how do we help them to get a more biblically based view of sex?

5. Summarize Scanzoni's approach to sex education. What do you think of the quotation with which she ends the chapter? Are there other approaches to sex education which are as good or better than that of Scanzoni?

6. The author suggests that parents should have a good knowledge of sex including an acquaintance with the functioning and correct names for the various parts of the body. Presumably parents know something about sex (or they wouldn't be parents), but where can they get more specific information? Can you refer to specific books or other sources of information?

CONCLUDING COMMENTS

Scanzoni assumes that sex education is a responsibility of parents and that such training should take place in the home. Do you think the church has any responsibility in this area? If so, what is the church's role either in giving sex education directly and/or helping parents to do a better job of sex education? Try to be specific as you think about this, and make application to your own church.

Chapter 10
Sex, Inside and Outside Marriage
David A. Seamands

In this very practical and encouraging final chapter, David Seamands tackles the issues of masturbation, sex outside of marriage, and sex as it was meant to be within marriage. Several times in this chapter the author mentions love which is the basis of truly satisfying sex. Read 1 Corinthians 13 to remind yourself of God's portrait of love. Then read John 15:10–13. Do you have problems with "sex, inside and outside of marriage"? How could your sexual experiences be more in keeping with God's expectations for us?

MEETING TOGETHER

1. Begin your group by reading John 15:10–13 aloud. What might this have to do with sex?

2. What should be the Christian attitude towards masturbation? Do you agree or disagree with Seamands' conclusion? Give reasons for your answer. Would you accept the author's view that masturbation "is possible without fantasy or lust, so that it cannot simply be taken for granted that it is always a lustful and thus a sinful act"? How would you counsel with someone who has a masturbation problem?

3. What is the difference between fornication and adultery? Ask different group members to look up and read the verses mentioned in the footnotes of Seamand's chapter: Matthew 15:19; Mark 7:21; Acts 15:20, 29; 21:15; Romans 1:29; 1 Corinthians 6:13, 18; 10:8; 15:1; 2 Corinthians 12:21; Galatians 5:19; Ephesians 5:3; Colossians 3:5; 1 Thessalonians 4:3. What do these verses tell us about what God thinks of fornication and adultery?

4. According to Seamands, how can a couple avoid premarital intercourse? Do you have other suggestions for sexual control before marriage? What about extramarital intercourse? How can this be avoided? Try to give practical answers, remembering that sex outside of marriage is a big problem for many people—perhaps for others in your group. Perhaps for you!

5. Do you agree that sex within marriage is something to celebrate? How do you respond to the author's suggestion that within marriage "anything that is physically enjoyable, emotionally fulfilling, and mutually agreeable is morally right. The important phrase here is 'mutually agreeable' since at the heart

of married love is respect for the partner's wishes and a desire to please. Outside of this governing principle there are no taboos, no restrictions except those of loving and caring about the other person"?

CONCLUDING COMMENT

This chapter has discussed the problems of masturbation, fornication and adultery, ending with a strong positive statement about the joys and beauty of sex within marriage. Is your church dealing with these issues—giving people a healthy view of sex and helping them to avoid "second best" types of sexual experience? What could the church be doing to help Christians better understand the secrets of our sexuality? What could you be doing? Sex, as created and described by God is to be enjoyed —not just as a spark, but as a flame!